2 *in* 1

Leaving Something Behind:

A Brief Examination of a Text
and
A Few Bible-Based Poems and Sayings

By

THOMAS WILLIAMS, PhD

Elder, Pastor, and Bible-Teacher

1st WORLD
PUBLISHING

2 *in* 1

Leaving Something Behind

Thomas Williams

© Thomas Williams 2011

Published by 1stWorld Publishing
P.O. Box 2211, Fairfield, Iowa 52556
tel: 641-209-5000 • fax: 866-440-5234
web: www.1stworldpublishing.com

First Edition

LCCN: 2011926577
SoftCover ISBN: 978-1-4218-8606-0
HardCover ISBN: 978-1-4218-8607-7
eBook ISBN: 978-1-4218-8608-4

This material has been written and published solely for educational purposes. The author and the publisher shall have neither liability nor responsibility to any person or entity with respect to any loss, damage or injury caused or alleged to be caused directly or indirectly by the information contained in this book.

Contents

BOOK I

BOOK II

"Study to show thyself approved unto God,
a workman that needed not to be ashamed,
rightly dividing the word of truth."

(2nd Timothy 2:15)

Book I

In Memory Of

Charlie Mack Williams ("daddy"), Bishop Carey Cornish
Bowles ("uncle"), Beanie Mae Wilson Brown ("grandma"),
Matthew David Davis ("a fine boy"), Dr. Audrey Qualls
Payne, Dr. Ursula M. Delworth ("mother"), Mother Verlene
Gamble Polite and Daddy Emerette Luckie Polite, Bishop
John Arthur Henderson, Bishop William S. Geddis, Elect
Lady Evangelist Josephine Hart ("a powerful woman of
God"), Elder Solomon Joseph Sanders ("my first pastor-of-
record"), and Bishop S.C. Johnson ("my grandfather-in-the-
faith")…a few people who I loved, admired, and respected.

Acknowledgements

I thank and praise the Lord for anointing, blessing, and encouraging me to write this book...thank you Jesus!

I thank the Lord for my precious mother, Alice Williams; my aunt, Sarah Rosa Wilson Bowles; my dear brother, Bishop Robert D. Taylor (and his wife Stella), Mother Patricia Weaver, Mother Rosa Walker, Harold Dee Wright, and a host of others for their love, support and prayers.

I thank the Lord for how Bishop Quinton T. Wallace encouraged me "to hold on to your dream." Thank you, Daddy Wallace!

I thank the Lord for my precious brothers and sisters because they mean so much to me!

I thank the Lord for my precious nieces, nephews, and students. I count all of you as my sons and daughters.

I feel so honored to have two nephews, who carry my first name. A part of me will live on through them.

I thank the Lord for Halifax Medical Center's Cardiac Rehabilitation staff (Jerome "Jerry" Boggs, Lauren Dack, Sherry Jarell, Lisa Sixma, and Sandra Tomasello) for working with me during my recovery, especially my precious brother ("daddy"), Michael Steward Jr. May God bless and keep you.

I want to thank Richard V. Campagna, Esq. and Sadie May for reading an earlier version of this project. I pray that God bless you for being a blessing me!

A special thank you goes out to Embry-Riddle Aeronautical University for letting me use their computers and library.

I pray that the "God of the whole earth" (Isaiah 54:5) bless you as you read this project and share what you learn with others.

Dedication

My father told me to "give something back to the community," whereas my uncle and former pastor told me to "leave something behind." Thus, I wrote this book with a charge from them.

The apostle Paul declared, "In the mouth of two or three witnesses shall every word be established" (2nd Corinthians 13:1). Their words were established, and, as such, I wrote "Leaving Something Behind: A Brief Examination of a Text."

I dedicate this book to my immediate family and to the memory of my precious late father, Charlie Mack Williams; my uncle and former pastor, the late Bishop Dr. Carey Cornish Bowles; my grandfather-in-the-faith, the late Bishop S.C. Johnson; and to a man who I was pleased to call "daddy", the late Emerette Luckie Polite. This book is a way to leave my voice in the earth.

The Selection Process

The Old Testament (OT) has 39 books, whereas the New Testament (NT) has 27. Collectively, we have 66 books in our English Bible. Out of 39 OT books, 72 percent (n=28) of them have a 3:16. The New Testament, on the other hand, has 27 books and 21 of them (78%) have a 3:16. Thus, I used 28 OT scriptures and 21 NT scriptures, which will be the focus of our discussion. Unless otherwise indicated, Bible references will come from the King James Version (1611 edition). I did not use the Apocrypha or The Lost Books of the Bible, as I relied on "authorized canon."

Forward

In preparing to teach a text, use your discretion, freedom, and power. Because everyone (teacher) is different, your approach will mirror your personality, what you want to teach (share with your class), and how you plan to share it. For instance, someone may teach the application, history, or theory of a text, whereas another person will examine a text in light of the zeitgeist (spirit of the times).

A person's training and experience will influence how he or she prepares and looks at a text. Thus, a biblical historian may examine a text in light of social mores and how a particular text is relevant in modern times.

Presenting a text is another story. For instance, one has to consider how much "time" he or she will actually have to preach, share, talk, or teach. For the sake of discussion, let us assume that I was invited to be a speaker at XYZ bible conference and had 30 minutes to present Matthew 3:16: the time factor, in itself, will influence how I prepare.

The bottom line is: (1) you can approach a text any way you like, but keep it rooted and grounded in scripture, (2) be mindful of how much time you have to present, (3) use biblical history but not at the expense of, nor in place of scripture, and (4) use supporting scriptures to help clarify your position.

For this project, I kept my study rooted and grounded in scripture. I used outside sources and consulted the Lord. As Solomon declared, "In all thy ways acknowledge him, and he shall direct thy path" (Proverbs 3:6). He did!

As I prepared this manuscript, I documented my thoughts, was flexible and sensitive to the voice of the Lord. I recognized my limitations (weaknesses), built on my strengths, and saved drafts of the document in order to monitor my progress and make [the] appropriate corrections.

As a student-of-scripture, I try to give my audience something to think about and to stir up their pure minds (2nd Peter 3:1).

From one teacher's heart to another, as you prepare your text, think on these things:

1. Will you be the "sage on the stage" or the "guide on the side?"

2. How much time will you have to prepare for and present the text?

3. Who is your targeted audience?

4. What are your teaching goals and objectives?

5. How will you present them?

6. What do you want your audience to learn and take home?

7. Did you consider your audience's age, attention span, prior Bible knowledge, background, gender, race, and learning styles?

8. How will you assess your audience's level of functioning and willingness to learn?

9. Will you have to make reasonable accommodations for anyone in your audience with special needs? If so, how will you accommodate them?

10. Which Bible translation or translations will you use?

11. How comfortable (knowledgeable) are you with the text?

12. Will you teach and share only what you know and believe?

As you "study to show thyself approved unto God" (1st Timothy 2:15), stay in his face (Luke 18:1; 1st Thessalonians 5:19), be flexible, docile (teachable), and like Jesus, "lowly in heart" (Matthew 11:28-30). Like Solomon, ask for "an understanding heart" (1st Kings 3:5-15), and if you need wisdom, ask for it (James 1:5). To use the words of the late Bishop William S. Geddis, **"Let the Lord lead you like Gideon."** I pray that the Spirit of Truth lead and guide you into all truth (John 16:13), as you preach, teach, and tell the truth!

In his service,

Thomas Williams   March 10, 2009

Daytona Beach, Florida

THE SCRIPTURES
(The Old Testament)

"Unto the woman he said, I will greatly multiply thy sorrow and thy conception; in sorrow thou shalt bring forth children; and thy desire shall be to thy husband, and he shall rule over thee".

(Genesis 3:16)

Introduction to Genesis 3:16

The first book of Torah talks about the fall of man and how sin came into the world (Romans 5: 12-21). God told Adam not to eat of the "tree of the knowledge of good and evil" (Genesis 2:16-17). In turn, he told his wife not to eat from the tree. When Adam told Eve not to eat from the tree is a mystery (Deuteronomy 29:29).

One day, when Adam was not around, the serpent struck up a conversation with Eve (3:6). According to 2nd Corinthians 11:3, "The serpent beguiled Eve by his cunning [ways]" (The Amplified New Testament). Instead of obeying her husband, Eve ate from the **tree of knowledge of good and evil** and gave a fruit to her husband. When Adam ate, he disobeyed God and sinned (3:11). Instantly, Adam's and Eve's eyes were opened, and they realized that they were naked. Adam and his wife made aprons and took cover (hid).

Examination of Genesis 3:16

In this passage, God questioned Eve and sentenced her for eating from the forbidden tree. Instead of owning and taking responsibility for her actions, Eve tried to take herself off the hook by saying, "The serpent beguiled me" (3:13). Adam blamed his wife (3:12), but the serpent had no one to blame (3:13).

Thought for Genesis 3:16

Don't blame me for what you do. "For every man shall bear his own burden" (Galatians 6:5).

Discussion Questions for Genesis 3:16

1. Define beguile.

2. What does the Bible say about the lust of the flesh and the lust of eyes?

3. What does the Bible say about the serpent?

4. What did Jesus say about the devil?

"Go, and gather the elders of Israel together, and say unto them, The LORD God of your fathers, the God of Abraham, of Isaac, and of Jacob, appeared unto me saying, I have surely visited you, and seen that which is done to you in Egypt."

(Exodus 3:16)

Introduction to Exodus 3:16

The second book of Torah calls to mind the birth of Moses and how the devil tried to destroy him in infancy (Exodus 1:15-16). God, however, intervened and spared his life.

Before Moses was born, the king of Egypt told all of the Egyptian midwives to kill all Hebrew boys at birth (Exodus 1:15-16). Because the midwives "feared God," they ignored the king's decree (Exodus 1:17). When God has his hand on your life, the devil cannot touch you. The scripture declares, "Touch not mine anointed, and do my prophets no harm" (1st Chronicles 16:22).

Moses' parents feared God and hid him for three months (2:1-2; Acts 7:20). When his mother saw that she could no longer hide him, she made "an ark of bulrushes" and put him in it (2:3).

One day when Pharaoh's daughter, Thermuthis, was bathing she saw an ark along the Nile (Josephus, Antiquities of the Jews 2.9.5). Out of curiosity, Thermuthis told (ordered) one of her maids to swim over and get it (Josephus, Antiquities of the Jews 2.9.6.). The maid swam over, got it, and brought the ark to her. As soon as Thermuthis opened the ark (basket) and looked at the Hebrew boy, she had compassion on him: she took him home and raised the boy as her own son (2:10). Thermuthis named the Hebrew boy Mouses, who the world knows as Moses (Josephus, Antiquities of the Jews 2.9.6).

Moses had the best of everything but did not forget where he came from. One day, he saw an Egyptian mistreat a Hebrew and killed him (2:11-12). After someone told pharaoh that Moses had killed an Egyptian, he "sought to kill him" (2:15). Moses ran for cover.

Moses went to Midian, met a woman, and got married. For work, he took care of his father-in-law's flock (3:1)." One day while he was taking care of the wild stock, "an angel of the LORD appeared to him in a burning bush" (3:1-2). The burning bush caught Moses' eye and he went to "check it out." That day, God spoke to Moses and told him to go to pharaoh and tell him to let his people go.

Examination of Exodus 3:16

God sent Moses to the then-pharaoh (in Egypt). Because Moses was meek (Number 12:3), he asked God, "Who am I that I should go to Pharaoh and lead the Israelites out of Egypt" (3:11, New American Bible)? God's reply was, "Certainly, I will be with thee" (3:12, KJV). Moses took comfort in God's response, was willing to obey, but had another question. "When I go to the Israelites and say to them, 'The God of your fathers has sent me to you,' if they ask me, "What is his name?' what am I to tell them" (3:13, New American Bible)? God told Moses to tell them, "I AM sent me to you" (3:14, New American Bible).

Concerning I AM, Jesus said, "I am the living bread" (John 6:51), "I am the light of the world" (John 8:12), "I am the door" (John 10:9), and "I am the good shepherd" (John 10:11). With humility and grace, Jesus declared, "I am the son of God" (10:36), "I am the way, truth, and the life" (John 14:6), "I am the true vine" (John 15:1), and "I am the king of the Jews" (John 19:2). In the Book of Revelation, Y'Shua (Jesus) said, "I am Alpha and Omega" (1:8, 11; 22:13), "I am the first and the last" (Revelation 1:17), "I am he that liveth, and was dead" (Revelation 1:18), and "I am alive for evermore" (Revelation 1:18). Jesus is the great I AM!

Jesus did not operate in a vacuum, as he declared, "I am not alone" (John 8:16), "I am from above" (John 8:23), "I am one that bear witness of myself" (John 8:18), and "I and my father are one" (John 10:30). The Book of Revelation says, "The testimony of Jesus is the spirit of prophecy" (19:6).

In our text, God sent Moses to the elders of Israel…The LORD, the God of your fathers, the God of Abraham, Isaac and Jacob, has appeared to me and said: I am concerned about you and about the way you are being treated in Egypt" (3:13, New American Bible).

I believe that God sent Moses to Pharaoh in order to keep a "promise" that he made with Abram. God told Abram, "Know for certain that your descendants shall be aliens in a land not their own, where they shall be enslaved and oppressed for four hundred years. But I will bring judgment on the nation they must serve, and in the end they will depart with great wealth" (Genesis 15:13-14, New American Bible). Thus, when God brought Israel from out of Egypt (Hosea 11:1), he kept his word .As the scripture declares, "God is not a man, that he should lie; neither the son of man, that he should repent" (Numbers 23:19).

Thought for Exodus 3:16

God watches and listens to us. "For the eyes of the Lord are upon the righteous, and his ears are opened unto our cry" (Psalms 34:15).

Discussion Questions for Exodus 3:16

1. What is a pharaoh?

2. Which pharaoh did Moses go to?

3. Who were the elders?

4. What is an elder?

5. Who were Moses parents?

"And the priest shall burn them upon the altar: it is the food of the offering made by fire for a sweet savour: all the fat is the LORD'S."

(Leviticus 3:16)

Introduction to Leviticus 3:16

Leviticus is the third book of Torah and is the book of the priests and offerings. The sons (descendants) of Levi, who were the priests and Levites, replaced the first born males in Israel (Number 3).

Before Torah, Abel brought an offering to the LORD (Genesis 4:4). When Noah came out of the ark, he built an altar and offered burnt sacrifices to the Lord (Genesis 8:20-21). Jethro, who was Moses' father-in-law, presented a burnt offering before the Lord (Exodus 18:12). God told Abraham to present Isaac as a burnt offering (Genesis 18:2-14), but when God saw Abraham's obedience, he let Isaac live!

After Torah was given, "sacrifice was the accepted mode of worship" (Langston, 1991). The sacrifice was connected to the tent of meeting and the temple.

In Messiah, the "physical sacrifice became unnecessary" (Langston, 1991) because "Christ died for our sins according to the scriptures" (1st Corinthians 15:3) and "bore our sins in his own body on the tree" (1st Peter 2:24). Jesus suffered once for sins (1st Peter 3:18) and willingly gave Himself up for our sins (Galatians 1:4, The Amplified New Testament). With grace from the Lord, we must present our body as "a living sacrifice, holy, and acceptable unto God" (Romans 12:1).

Examination of Leviticus 3:16

There were 5 types of offerings: the burnt offering (Leviticus 1), the meat offering (Leviticus 2), the peace offering

(Leviticus 3), the sin offering (Leviticus 4), and the trespass offering (Leviticus 5-7). In our brief discussion, I will talk about the peace offering.

There were stipulations for presenting and eating the peace offering. For instance, the peace offering (animal) could not have a blemish or defect (3:1, 6). The man who brought the peace offering to the priest laid his hands on it and killed the peace offering at the door of the tabernacle of congregation. Then, the priest presented the peace offering to the Lord. The children of Israel ate a portion of the peace offering (animal) but could not eat its fat or drink its blood (Leviticus 17:6, 10-14).

In Messiah, a peace offering is not required, as he (Jesus) is our peace (Ephesians 2:14). In regards to peace, Jesus preached peace (Acts 10:36; Ephesians 2:17), and if God called you to preach, you will preach the gospel of peace (Isaiah 52:7; Romans 10:15). According to the apostle Paul, peace is a fruit (manifestation) of the spirit (Galatians 5:22-23). As believers, we must "seek peace" (Psalm 34:14) and "follow peace with all men" (Hebrews 12:14). God is the author (originator) of peace (1ˢᵗ Corinthians 14:33; Hebrews 13:20). As believers, we must let (allow) the peace of God rule in our hearts (Colossians 3:15), and remember that "That the kingdom of God is …in righteousness and peace, and joy in the Holy Ghost" (Romans 14:17).

Thought for Leviticus 3:16

Try to get along with other people. "If it be possible, as much as lieth in you, live peaceably with all men" (Romans 12:18).

Discussion Questions for Leviticus 3:16

1. What was an offering?

2. What was the tabernacle?

3. What was the door of the tabernacle?

"And Moses numbered them according to the word of the LORD, as he was commanded."

(Numbers 3:16)

Introduction to Numbers 3:16

Numbers is the forth book of Torah: part of the book talks about Levi and how Moses counted Israel three times. Moreover, Levi was Israel's third son and one of the 12 tribes of Israel. Levi "belonged" to the Lord and "replaced" the first born males in Israel (Numbers 3), as he stood up when Moses said, "Who is on the Lord's side" (Exodus 32:26)?

When he was of age, Levi got married and had 3 sons: Gershon, Kohath, and Merari (Numbers 3:17). Out of Levi came the priests (sons of Aaron) and Levites (assistants-to-the priest). The tribe of Levi is among the 144,000 that was sealed (Revelation 7:7).

This chapter talks about how Moses counted the children of Israel. For instance, God told Moses and Aaron to "take a census of the whole Israelite community" …and to "record them by their groups, from the age of twenty years up, all those who are able to bear arms" (Numbers 1:2-3, Tanakh). Out of the 11 tribes, there were 603,550 men (Numbers 1:45, 2:32) who were able to bear arms (go to war). This was the first census.

Examination of Numbers 3:16

God told Moses "to number all of the children of Levi …from a month old and upward" (Numbers 3:15). Moses obeyed the

Lord God and counted 22,000 (Levites) males who were one month and older (Numbers 3:39). Moses did not, however, count any girls, women, or boys less than a month old. This was the second census.

On another occasion, the LORD told Moses to count all of the first born males in ancient Israel who were at least a month old (Numbers 3:40-43). Moses counted 22, 273 first born Israelite males. This was the third census.

Thought for Numbers 3:16

The scripture says, "The LORD shall count, when he writeth up the people, that this man was born there. Selah" (Psalm 87:6). In the United States, we take a census every ten years.

Discussion Questions for Numbers 3:16

1. What is a census?

2. What is a command?

3. What is the theme of the book of Numbers?

"And unto the Reubenites and unto the Gadities I gave from Gilead even unto the river Arnon half the valley, and the border of even unto the river Jabbok, which is the border of the children of Ammon."

(Deuteronomy 3:16)

Introduction to Deuteronomy 3:16

According to the late Bishop Carey C. Bowles, Deuteronomy is the **"book-of-the-repeat"** and is the last book of Torah. Under the leadership of Moses, the armies of Israel defeated king Og and king Sihon: thus, Israel took their cities, land,

and killed its inhabitants (Psalm 78; 136).

Before Israel crossed Jordan, the children of Reuben, of Gad, and of Manassah went to Moses, Eleazer, and the princes of the congregation and told them that they did not want to leave Jazar and Gilead. After much discussion and careful consideration, Moses told them that they had to cross Jordan and help their brothers drive out her enemies and subdue the land of Canaan. "Then afterward ye shall return, and be guiltless before the LORD, and before all Israel; and this land shall be your possession before the LORD" (32:22). The children of Reuben, of Gad, and of Manassah said, "Thy servants will do as my lord commandeth" (Numbers 32:25).

The Reubenites were descendants of Israel's oldest son, Reuben. Like his brothers, he hated Joseph (Genesis 37:3-11) but did not want to kill him (Genesis 37:20-21). On the other hand, the Gadities were the "sons" of Gad, who was Israel's 7th son through Leah. Manassah was Joseph's youngest son. Israel adopted Manassah and Ephraim when he said, "They shall be mine" (Genesis 48:5). Reuben, Gad, and Manassah were tribes in Israel.

Examination of Deuteronomy 3:16

This passage is just a "repeat" of what Moses told the children of Reuben, of Gad, and of the ½ tribe of Manassah (Numbers 32). Once they helped their brother conquer and subdue the land of Canaan, Reuben, Gad, and the ½ tribe of Manassah could go back to Jazar and Gilead. If they reneged, Reuben, Gad, and Manassah had to stay in Canaan. Israel crossed Jordan under Joshua's administration (Joshua 1:12-15).

Thought for Deuteronomy 3:16

To use the words of the late Bishop William S. Geddis, "Let the Lord led you like Gideon." The scripture declares,

"The steps of a good man are ordered by the LORD: and he delighteth in his way" (Psalm 37:23). Thus, let the Lord led you from earth to glory.

Discussion Questions for Deuteronomy 3:16

1. Where is the river Arnon?

2. Who were the children of Ammon?

3. Define border.

"That the waters which came down from above stood and rose up upon an heap very far from the city Adam, that is beside Zaretan: and those that came down toward the salt sea plain, even the salt sea, failed, and were cut off: and the people passed over right against Jericho."

(Joshua 3:16)

Introduction to Joshua 3:16

Joshua was the son of Nun and [he] probably was born a slave in Egypt. He was one of the 12 spies (Numbers 13:1-17), a servant (Exodus 33:11), and one who was full of the spirit (Deuteronomy 34:9). Joshua's name means "Jehovah-saves."

Before he got promoted (died), Moses asked the LORD to set a man over the congregation (Numbers 27:16) because he did not want Israel to be like a sheep without a shepherd (Numbers 27:17). God answered his prayer by selecting Joshua as "the man." Out of obedience, Moses laid his hands on him (Joshua) and said, "Be strong and of good courage: for thou shalt bring the children of Israel into the land which I sware unto them: and I will be with thee" (Deuteronomy 31:23).

Moses died and Israel mourned for him for 30-days

(Deuteronomy 34:8-9). On the 31ˢᵗ day, God told Joshua, "…
arise, go over this Jordan" (Joshua 1:2). In order to encourage
him, God declared, "…as I was with Moses, so will I be with
thee" and "only be thou strong and very courageous" (Joshua
1:7, 18). Joshua was her (Israel's) pastor for 25 years (Joshua
24:29).

Examination of Joshua 3:16

The time came for Israel to cross Jordan. As her pastor, Joshua
got the priests and the people ready to pass over to Jericho.
The priests walked to the edges of the river and put their feet
in the water. As soon as their feet touched the water, God
divided the water. "He rebuked the sea, and maketh it dry,
and dried up the river" (Nahum 1:4; see also Psalm 106:9).
The priests in turned walked into the middle of the Jordan
and stood there until all of the children of Israel passed thru
it. After Israel crossed over, the priests joined their brothers.
Then, the Lord God returned the water back to its normal
state.

Thought for Joshua 3:16

God makes a way out of what we call no-way. "…for with
God all things are possible" (Mark 10:27).

Discussion Questions for Joshua 3:16

1. Which tribe was Joshua from?

2. How old was Joshua when he became Israel's pastor?

3. How old was Joshua when he died?

4. What was Joshua' birth name?

"But Ehud made him a dagger which had two edges, of a cubit length; and he did gird it under his raiment upon his right thigh."

(Judges 3:16)

Introduction to Judges 3:16

The Book of Judges "contains the history of Biblical judges who helped rule and guide the ancient Israelites" (Book of Judges, Wikipedia, the free encyclopedia). God raised up judges and rulers to get Israel back on track.

It seems as if the children of Israel did not learn from history. Time and time again, she fell into apostasy. The Lord punished her, and in anguish, she cried out to Him and he delivered her. The psalmist said, "Many are the afflictions of the righteous but the Lord delivers them out of them all" (Psalm 34:19). Thus, God raised up a "deliver" (2:16, 18), but when he died, she went back to her old ways. "Righteousness exalted a nation but sin is a reproach to any people" (Proverbs 14:34).

The LORD left people in the land to "prove" Israel (3:1-4). Instead of driving them out, she (Israel) married their sons and daughters (3:6) and served their gods (3:7). God told Israel not to intermarry (Deuteronomy 7:1-4) and serve other gods (Exodus 20:3-5; 34:14; Deuteronomy 6:14). Israel, however, did not listen (see Psalm 106:34-39).

God was provoked by her actions and sold them (the nation of Israel) into slavery (3:7-8). In her distress, she cried out and God raised up a deliverer—Othniel (3:9). Under Othniel's leadership, Israel defeated her enemy and had rest for forty years (3:10-11). When Othniel died, she went back to her old ways (3:12).

This time, she was taken into captivity by king Eglon and

was in bondage, slavery, or involuntary servitude for 18 years. Eglon was a Moabite and a descendant of Lot (Genesis 19:37). As a manner of custom, Israel cried out to the Lord, he heard her, and raised up a deliverer—Ehud.

Ehud was from the tribe of Benjamin and was one of the five so-called "Great Judges" (Book of Judges, JewishEncyclopedia.com).The five Great Judges were Ehud (3:12-30), Deborah (Judges 4-5), Gideon (Judges 6:1-8:32), Jephthah (Judges 10:6-12:7), and Samson (Judges 13-16).

Examination of Judges 3:16

Ehud killed king Eglon. As he walked towards the king, Ehud told him, "I have a secret errand unto thee, O king" (3:19). No doubt, Eglon was excited and wanted to hear what Ehud had to say. To make sure that no one heard their conversation, Eglon made his men leave his chambers. After his men left, Ehud seized the moment and stabbed the king in the stomach with a dagger. Quietly, Ehud got up, locked the king's door, and went home. Under Ehud's leadership, Israel rose up, defeated her enemy [the Moabites], and lived in peace for eighty years (3:30). Our legal system would call Ehud a cold blooded murderer ...God did not (2:16, 18)!

Thought for Judges 3:16

Hating your brother is tantamount to killing him (1st John 3:15). "Thou shalt not kill" (Exodus 20:13).

Discussion Questions for Judges 3:16

1. Who were the Canaanites, Hittites, Amorites, Perizzites, Hivites, and Jebusites?

2. Who were the Philistines, and what did they do against Israel?

3. Of the five "Great Judges," who ruled Israel the longest?

"When Ruth came to her mother-in-law, Naomi asked, 'How did it go, my daughter'?"

(Ruth 3:16, NIV)

Introduction to Ruth 3:16

This is the first book in the Bible named after a woman. Due to famine in Bethlehem Elimelech took his wife, Naomi, and his sons, Mahlon and Chilion, to Moab.

While in Moab, Elimelech died. After his death, his sons got married. Mahlon married Ruth, whereas Chilion married Orpah. Ten years later, the boys died. Naomi lost her husband and her sons.

The Bible says that Ruth was a Moabitess. She married a Jew (1:4) and had a good relationship with her mother-in-law. The Bible, however, does not tell us how she met Mahlon, why she married him, or how old she was when she got married. Ruth lost her father-in-law, her husband, and brother-in-law. No doubt, her grief was as thick as a dark cloud.

After the death of her sons, Naomi and Ruth went back to Bethlehem but Oprah stayed in Moab. In order to survive, Ruth gleaned corn in Boaz's field (Deuteronomy 24:19-22) and received a portion of the third year tithe (Deuteronomy 26:12).

When Boaz saw Ruth, she caught his eye, and he took an interest in her (2:4-6). He instantly liked her and was pleased with how well she treated her mother-in-law (2:10-12). Everyone knew that Ruth had a good relationship with her mother-in-law, Naomi. Ruth found grace in Boaz's eyes. He protected her (2:9), made sure that she had water to drink

(2:9), food to eat (2:14), and barley to take home (2:15-19).

In keeping with the custom of the day, Ruth could get married and have children but [she] needed a kinsman redeemer. The kinsman redeemer would keep her late husband's name alive (Genesis 38:7-18). The Bible does not say this, but Ruth probably was a convert to Judaism or a stranger who adopted the Hebrew way of life.

There were two kinsmen redeemers (2:1; 4). The first kinsmen redeemer did not want to marry Ruth out of fear of losing his own inheritance (4:6). That left Boaz, who was a relative on Ruth's husband side of the family (2:1).

Boaz redeemed and married Ruth. They had Obed (4:17). When Obed got married, he and his wife gave birth to Jesse, who later became David's father (4:22; 1st Samuel 16:1-13). When David took Bathsheba, they had Solomon (2nd Samuel 12:24). Thus, Ruth was Jesse' grandmother, David' great-grandmother, and Solomon's great-great grandmother.

Examination of Ruth 3:16

After spending the night at Boaz' feet on the threshing floor, Ruth got up early in the morning and went home. Boaz told her to leave early in the morning because he did not want anyone to see Ruth leave his house. Before she left, Boaz gave Ruth six measures of barley to take home. When Ruth got home, her mother-in-law (Naomi) asked her about her affairs. As a faithful daughter, Ruth told Naomi how Boaz had blessed her (3:11-15).

Thought for Ruth 3:16

Love is the gift that keeps giving. "Let brotherly love continue" (Hebrews 13:1).

Discussion Questions for Ruth 3:16

1. What does the Bible say about the daughter-in-law and the mother-in-law?

2. What does the Bible say about intermarriage?

3. If you were married, how would you treat your mother-in-law?

4. If you are married, how do you treat your mother-in-law?

5. Where is Mt. Nebo?

6. Who was Boaz's father?

"Then Eli called Samuel, and said, Samuel my son. And he answered, Here am I"

(1ˢᵗ Samuel 3:16)

Introduction to 1ˢᵗ Samuel 3:16

Hannah was barren and wanted children. One day she prayed and made a vow. She said, "...if thou wilt indeed look on the affliction of thine handmaid, and remember me, and not forget thine handmaid, but wilt give unto thine hand-maid a man child, then I will give him unto the LORD all the days of his life, and there shall no razor come upon his head "(3:11). The Lord heard her cry and blessed her to have Samuel (3:19-20).

After Hannah weaned Samuel (1:24) and offered a sacrifice, she took him to Eli (1ˢᵗ Samuel 1:26-28), who raised him in the temple. "Train a lad in the way he ought to go; He will not swerve from it even in old age" (Proverbs 22:5, Tanakh). Because Hannah gave Samuel to the Lord, he (the Lord) blessed her to have more children (2:20-21).

One night when Samuel was sleeping, the Lord called him. Thinking that it was Eli, he ran to his quarters, and said, "Here am I: for thou callest me." Eli told him, "I did not call you: lie down." Once again, the Lord called Samuel and he ran back to Eli's quarters. When Eli perceived that the Lord had called Samuel, he told Samuel, "Go, lie down: and it shall be, if he call thee, that thou shalt say, Speak, LORD; for thy servant heareth" (3:9). Samuel went back to his room and the Lord called him again. This time, Samuel said, "Speak Lord, for your servant hears." When the Lord God got his attention, the Lord told Samuel how he was going to punish Eli and his two sons (1ˢᵗ Samuel 2:27-36).

According to Flavius Josephus, God called Samuel when he was 12 years old (Antiquities 5.10.4). According to the gospel of James, God called Mary to be the mother of Jesus when she was 14 years old. God told Jeremiah, "Before I created you in the womb, I selected you; before you were born, I consecrated you; I appointed you a prophet concerning the nations" (Jeremiah 1:4-5, Tanakh). Moreover, God called John the Baptist to be the forerunner (Isaiah 40:3) and messenger of Messiah (Malachi 3:1) before he was born (Luke 1:5-25, 57-80). To fulfill scripture, God got into a body (Psalm 40:6-8; Isaiah 35:3-6; 53; Zechariah 12:10; John 1:1, 14) and purchased the church with his own blood (Acts 20:28; 1ˢᵗ John 3:16). The apostle Paul was consecrated (by God) to preach the gospel before he was born (Galatians 1:15), and God called me when I was 8 years old.

Examination of 1ˢᵗ Samuel 3:16

The next day, Eli confronted Samuel saying, "What did the Lord tell you? Tell me, and do not hold anything back." Moreover, "God do so to thee, and more also, if thou hide anything from me" (3:17). Initially, Samuel was afraid to tell

Eli what God had told him (3:15). Out of fear and obedience, he spilled his guts (3:18).

Thought for 1ˢᵗ Samuel 3:16

Always say yes to Jesus. "To day if ye hear his voice, harden not your heart, as in the provocation" (Hebrews 3:15).

Discussion Questions for 1ˢᵗ Samuel 3:16

1. How many children did Hannah have?

2. How long did Eli judge Israel?

3. How did Eli die?

"Her husband, however, went with her, weeping behind her all the way to Bahurim. Then, Abner said to him, 'Go back home!' So he went back"

(2ⁿᵈ Samuel 3:16, NKJV)

Introduction to 2ⁿᵈ Samuel 3:16

The books of 1ˢᵗ Samuel and 2ⁿᵈ Samuel bears the prophet's [Samuel's] name. God used Samuel to anoint Saul (1ˢᵗ Samuel 10) and David (1ˢᵗ Samuel 16:1-13).

God was Israel's first king, but she rejected him in order to be like the other nations (1ˢᵗ Samuel 8:4-22). God suffered Saul to be her first [human] king (Deuteronomy 17:14-15; 1ˢᵗ Samuel 9; 10; and Acts 13:21), followed by David (1ˢᵗ Samuel 16:1-13; Acts 13:21) and Solomon (2ⁿᵈ Chronicles 1:7-9).

About David

David was a youth when he was anointed king of Israel (1ˢᵗ

Samuel 16:1-13). He became king of Israel when he was 30 and ruled for forty years (2nd Samuel 5:4). David was a shepherd, a musician, and a man after God's own heart (1st Samuel 16:19; 1st Samuel 16:16-23; 1st Samuel 13:14; Acts 13:22). David was courageous, good looking, and well-built (1st Samuel 17:14; 1st Samuel 16:19; 17:34-36).

David killed Uriah and took his wife (2nd Samuel 11; 12:9). Torah says, "Thou shalt not kill" (Exodus 20:13), and "Thou shalt not commit adultery" (Exodus 20:14). When David sinned against Uriah, he committed capital offenses worthy of death (Genesis 9:6; Revelation 13:10; Deuteronomy 5:17; Leviticus 20:10). The Lord, however, forgave David and let him live (2nd Samuel 12:13). We learn from David's experience that "your sin will find you out" (Numbers 32:23), as there is nothing hidden that won't be revealed (Mark 4:22; Luke 8:17).

Examination of 2nd Samuel 3:16

When Saul and Jonathan died, David cried (2nd Samuel 1:11-17). David knew that Saul hated and wanted to kill him (1st Samuel 18-20), but he never retaliated (1st Samuel 24:3-22; 26-9-11). When David had the opportunity to kill his father-in-law (Saul), he would not touch God's anointed (1st Samuel 24:10; 26:9-11; 1st Chronicles 16:22).

After the death of Saul, Abner asked David to make a pact with him. "If you make it, I will help you bring all Israel over to your side" (2nd Samuel 3:12-13-Tanakh). David made a pact with Abner because he wanted his wife back (1st Samuel 18:20-28). While David was on the run, his father-in-law, Saul, gave his wife, Michal, to Phalti, and she became his wife (1st Samuel 25:44).

In order to get his wife back, David sent a messenger to Ish-bosheth (who was his brother-in-law). The messenger told

Ish-bosheth that he (David) wanted his wife (Michal) back. Ish-bosheth sent for his sister, Michal, and made her go with David. In turn, David and his wife went home. Phalti, who was Michal's husband, cried and followed them.

Thought for 2nd Samuel 3:16

Sometimes, innocent people get hurt. "They that sow in tears shall reap in joy."

(Psalm 126:5)

Discussion Questions for 2nd Samuel 3:16

1. How many wives did David have?

2. Did Mickal and David get married?

3. Did Mickal and David have any children?

4. Did Paltiel know that Mickal was espoused to David?

"Two women who were harlots came to the king, and stood before him."

(1st Kings 3:16, NKJV)

Introduction to 1st Kings 3:16

When David died, his son, Solomon, became king of Israel. Solomon was the last king to rule a united kingdom. Solomon was her king for 40 years (1st Kings 11:42).

A piece of the scripture says ... "Then came there two women." The text is tacit (silent) as to who those women were, and where they came from. Moreover, the Bible says nothing in regards to their age, nationality, or if it were customary for women to come before a king.

Another part of the scriptures says, "…that were harlots?" What was a harlot in that day? Who knew that those women were harlots, and how did they know?

In regards to harlots, Judah's daughter-in-law, Tamar, "played the harlot" (Genesis 38:24), Rahab was a harlot (Joshua 6:17; Hebrews 11:31), and Samson had sex with a harlot in Gaza (Judges 16:1). The Tanakh said, "…he [Samson] met a whore and slept with her." Israel and Judah played the harlot (Jeremiah 3:6, 8). The prophet Hosea married a "wife of whoredom" (Hosea 1:2), and Sha'ul (the apostle Paul) said, "…he which is joined to an harlot is one body" (1st Corinthians 6:16). Solomon declared, "…he that keepeth company with harlots spendeth his substance" (Proverbs 29:3). There is nothing new up under the sun.

Examination of 1st Kings 3:16

Two women stood before the king but one of them wanted justice (1st Kings 3:17-28). In sum, two women (harlots) were sharing an apartment (to use our modern language). During the course of the night, one of the women rolled over and suffocated (killed) her newborn baby. The woman who lost her child stole the other woman's baby, arguing the next day that it was hers. Solomon's ruling and wisdom shock-up the then-known world.

Thought for 1st Kings 3:16

You cannot do it [whatever "it" is] on your own. "If any man lack wisdom, let him ask of God who giveth to all men liberally and upbraideth not" (James 1:5-6).

Discussion Questions for 1st Kings 3:16

1. How old was Solomon when he became king?

2. What did Solomon ask the Lord for?

3. Did the Lord answer his prayer?

4. Did Solomon get married?

5. How old was Solomon when he died?

"And he said, Thus saith the Lord, Make this valley full of ditches."

(2ⁿᵈ **Kings 3:16**)

Introduction to 2ⁿᵈ Kings 3:16

Ahab was king of Israel for 22 years, and when he died, his son, Jehoram became king. The scripture says, "Ahab ... reigned over Israel in Samaria [for] twenty and two years" (1ˢᵗ Kings 16:29). That he "did evil in the sight of the LORD" (1ˢᵗ Kings 16:30) and provoked him (1ˢᵗ Kings 16:33). When Ahab died, the king of Moab rose up against Israel (3:5). Mesha was the king of Moab (3:4) and a descendant of Lot (Genesis 19:37). Jehoram, however, was also Jezebel's son.

Because Jehoram felt that he needed help, he went to Jehoshaphat (king of Judah) and asked him to help him fight the Moabites. Jehoshaphat replied, "I will go. I will do what you do: my troops shall be your troops, my horses shall be your horses (2ⁿᵈ Kings 3:7, Tanakh)."

After traveling with their men and "horses" for seven days, the kings of Israel, of Judah, and of Edom ran out of water and felt that they and their "horses" were going to die (3:9). In distress Jehoram said, "The Lord brought these three kings together only to deliver them into the hands of Moab (2ⁿᵈ Kings 3:10, Tanakh)." Jehoshaphat's reply was, "Isn't there a prophet of the Lord here, through whom we may inquire of the Lord" (2nd Kings 3:11, Tanakh). A servant of the king of Israel (Jehoram) told Jehoshaphat (king of Judah) about Elisha (3:11). Instead of sending for him, the kings of Israel, Judah, and Edom went to his house. Going to Elisha's house was tantamount to the president of the United States coming to your house (home).

Examination of 2nd Kings 3:16

When Elisha saw Jehoram, he rebuked him. "What have you to do with me? Go to your father's prophets or your mother's prophets" (3:11, Tanakh). Out of respect for Jehoshaphat, Elisha told him what to do and that they would defeat their enemies…the Moabites.

Thought for 2nd Kings 3:16

Do not give in to defeat or to the enemy. "In all thy ways acknowledge him, and he shall direct thy paths" (Proverbs 3:6).

Discussion Questions for 2nd Kings 3:16

1. Who was Edom?

2. Who was Elisha?

3. Who were the Moabites?

"And the sons of Jehoiakim: Jeconiah his son, Zedekiah his son."

(1ˢᵗ Chronicle 3:16)

Introduction to 1ˢᵗ Chronicles 3:16

The first nine chapters in First Chronicles is a genealogy of Adam to the tribe of Benjamin. According to Carmody, Carmody, and Cohen (1988), 1ˢᵗ Chronicles [chapter] 3 "concentrates on the Davidic line, listing the offspring of David and Solomon (p.394)". It appears as if no women were [included] in the genealogy.

Solomon was one of David's 19 sons (1ˢᵗ Chronicles 3:1-7). When Solomon got married, he had about 15 sons (1ˢᵗ Chronicle 3:1-15). Josiah was one of Solomon's sons (1ˢᵗ Chronicles 3). David was Josiah's grandfather, Jesse was his great-grandfather, and Obed was his great-great grandfather.

Examination of 1ˢᵗ Chronicles 3:16

Josiah had four sons: Johana, Jehoiakim, Zedekiah, and Shallum (1ˢᵗ Chronicles 3:15). Josiah's son Jehoiakim became king of Judah when he was 25 years old: he reigned in Jerusalem for eleven years (2ⁿᵈ Kings 23:36). Jehoakim got married and had two sons: Jeconiah and Zedekiah. Jeconiah and Zedekiah were kings too.

Thought for 1ˢᵗ Chronicles 3:16

All of the kings of Israel and Judah were fathers. "Lo, children are a heritage of the Lord: and the fruit of the womb is his reward" (Psalm 127:3).

Discussion Question for 1ˢᵗ Chronicles 3:16

1. Who was Josiah's mother?

"And he made chains, as in the oracle, and put them on the heads of the pillars; and made an hundred pomegranates, and put them on the chains."

(2ⁿᵈ Chronicles 3:16)

Introduction to 2ⁿᵈ Chronicles 3:16

Before David died, he wanted to build a house (temple) for the Lord (2ⁿᵈ Samuel 7:1-12; 2ⁿᵈ Chronicles 6:7-8) but could not because he was a warrior with blood on his hands (1ˢᵗ Chronicles 22:7-10; 28:3). Knowing his heart, God told David that his "seed" would build him a house (2ⁿᵈ Samuel 7:13).

Solomon built the house for the LORD in Jerusalem in 1005 B.C. (Dictionary of Biblical Literacy). When he dedicated the temple, Solomon said, "But will God very deed dwell with man on earth? Behold, heaven and the heaven of heaven cannot contain thee; how much less this house which I built" (2ⁿᵈ Chronicles 6:18). As brother Stephens and Paul declared, "The Most High does not dwell in temples made with hands" (Acts 7:48; 17:24), as he dwells in his creation (2ⁿᵈ Corinthians 6:16).

Examination of 2ⁿᵈ Chronicles 3:16

Solomon built the house as he was instructed by his father (1ˢᵗ Chronicles 28:11-21). The LORD blessed him (Solomon) with a group of skilful men who willingly built the temple (1ˢᵗ Chronicles 28:21).

In this passage, a group of men made chains of gold and put them on the heads of the pillars. Pillars were columns that supported and held up the temple (Judges 16:25-29). The skilled men built pomegranates (artificial fruit ornaments) and put them on the golden chains.

Thought for 2nd Chronicles 3:16

"Thus saith the LORD, The heaven is my throne, and the earth is my footstool: where is the house that ye build unto me? And where is the place of my rest" (Isaiah 66:1)? Do you know?

Discussion Questions for 2nd Chronicles 3:16

1. How long did it take Solomon to build the temple?

2. What city was the temple built in?

3. Is there a difference between the temple and the tabernacle?

"After him repaired Nehemiah the son of Azbuk, the ruler of the half part of Beth-zur, unto the place over against the sepulchres of David, and to the pool that was made, and unto the house of the mighty."

(Nehemiah 3:16)

Introduction to Nehemiah 3:16

Hanani (a brother of Nehemiah) and "certain men of Judah" (1:2) told Nehemiah that the wall of Jerusalem was broken down and that the gates had been burned up (1:3; 7:2). Nehemiah was troubled by their report. Out of concern for Israel, Nehemiah prayed, looking to the Lord to touch the king's heart (1:11).

Nehemiah was king Artaxerxes' cupbearer. One day when he took the king his wine, Artaxerxes asked him, "Why is thy countenance sad" (2:1)? Before he answered the king's question, he prayed. Artaxerxe was the king of Persia from 465-425 B.C. (Halley, 1962). Nehemiah told him why he was sad and then asked for permission to go to Jerusalem in order to rebuild the wall and city gates (2:2-9). The king gave him leave and letters to travel. When Nehemiah arrived in Jerusalem, he rode around the city at night and surveyed the damage to the wall and gates.

Examination of Nehemiah 3:16

David was 70 years old when he died. The Bible says, "So David slept [died] with his fathers, and was buried in the city of David" (1st Kings 2:10). The city of David is Jerusalem or "the city of the great King" (Matthew 5:35).

Where David was buried was not a secret. David's tomb was close to Beth-zur, which was 13 miles south of Jerusalem. Brother Peter said, "Brothers, I can tell you confidently that the patriarch David died and was buried, and his tomb is here to this today" (Acts 2:29, New International Version [NIV]).

Shallum repaired the fountain gate (3:15). Then, Nehemiah, the son of Azbuk, "made repairs up to a point opposite the tombs of David, as far as the artificial pool of the House of the Heroes" (3:16, NIV). The "house of the mighty" is where David' warriors lived (2nd Samuel 23:8-39).

Thought for Nehemiah 3:16

Do not worry about a thing. Instead, "Cast thy burdens upon the Lord and he shall sustain thee: he shall never suffer the righteous to be removed" (Psalm 55:22). You cannot do it alone.

Discussion Questions for Nehemiah 3:16

1. What was the significance of the city wall?

2. Why was Judah taken into captivity?

3. What was a cupbearer?

"Or as an hidden untimely birth I had not been; as infants which never saw the light."

(Job 3:16)

Introduction to Job 3:16

Job was probably born and raised in Uz. Moreover, one could assume that Job lived under Torah because he offered up burnt offerings (Job 1:5; Leviticus 1-7).

Job is a good example of longsuffering (Galatians 5:22-23). If a person is patient, we say, "You have the patience of Job." Job was a type of Christ in that he was acquainted with sorrow and grief (Isaiah 53:1).

God tried Job and proved what was in his heart. One day God asked Satan, "Hast thou considered my servant Job" (1:8)? The devil retorted, "Doth Job fear God for nought" (1:9)? Satan knew that God had blessed Job (1:10) but said, "…touch all that he hath, and he will curse thee to thy face" (1:11). Because God knew and loved Job (Psalm 139:1-4), he made a way of escape for him (1st Corinthians 10:13).

In the process of time, Job's life took a turn- for-what-looked-like-the worse. Someone stole his oxen, asses, and camels. His servants were murdered, and his sons, daughters, and sheep died in a fire. In the midst of his sorrow, Job fell on his face and worshipped (1:20). Our precious brother said, "…the LORD gave, and the LORD hath taken away: blessed be the name of the LORD" (1:21). Job did not sin nor curse God to his face (1:22).

The devil tried to set Job up in order to have him stoned to death by the people. Leviticus 24:15-16 says, 'Whosoever curseth his God shall bear his sin. And he that blasphemeth the name of the LORD, he shall surely be put to death, and all the congregation shall certainly stone him." I am glad that Job did not curse God and die!

On another occasion, the LORD asked Satan, "Hast thou considered my servant Job" (2:3)? The devil retorted, "Skin for skin, yea, all that a man hath will he give for his life. But put forth thine hand now, and touch his bone and his flesh, and he will curse thee to thy face" (2:4-5). The LORD gave Satan permission to afflict Job, but he could not take his life (2:6).

The devil left the presence of the LORD and "smote him [Job] with sore boils from the sole of his foot unto his crown" (2:7). To add insult-to-injury, Job's wife said, "Curse your God and die" (2:9). Like Job, "Let us hold fast the profession of our faith without wavering" (Hebrews 10:23). Know that God is with us "even unto the end of the world "(Matthew 28:21). Job suffered loss but held on to his integrity (2:10). When his friends heard about his plight, they came to his aide.

Examination of Job 3:16

In his anguish, Job cursed the day that he was born but not the LORD. Job was sick, and, no doubt, in emotional anguish. As a father, he was grief-stricken and wanted to know why he did not die like a still born baby at birth. Although his soul was troubled, at no time did he blame God for his plight or so-called misfortune. No matter what we go through, we must always remember that "…the spirit is indeed willing but the flesh is weak" (Matthew 26:41).

Thought for Job 3:16

God is a deliverer. "Many are the afflictions of the righteous: but the Lord delivereth him out of them all" (Psalm 34:19).

Discussion Questions for Job 3:16

1. What is integrity?

2. Did Job do anything wrong?

3. At the end of his season of suffering, what did the Lord do for him?

"Length of days is in her hand; and in her left hand riches and honour."

(Proverbs 3:16)

Introduction to Proverbs 3:16

Was the book of Proverbs written to one of Solomon's son or to Israel? God told Moses, "Israel is my son, even my first born" (Exodus 4:31), and declared through the prophet Hosea, "When Israel was a child, then I loved him, and called my son out of Egypt" (Hosea 11:1). Since Solomon was the under shepherd (king) over God's people, he probably wrote to the house of Israel. Although Solomon was the wisest man in the then-known world, he still lost the kingdom (1ˢᵗ Kings 11:29-33). This passage represents 1 of Solomon's 3,000 proverbs (1ˢᵗ King 4:33).

Examination of Proverbs 3:16

Wisdom can make your life better (3:13) if you look for it. Wisdom is a person who cries at the gates (8:3) and calls men (8:4). A man who finds wisdom will be happy as she is precious, a rare commodity, and a tree of life. Whoever finds wisdom finds life and favor with the Lord (8:35).

"The LORD giveth wisdom" (2:6) and "layeth up sound wisdom for the righteous" (2:7). When Solomon asked for wisdom (1st Kings 3:5-12), he got it. If you need wisdom, ask for it in faith (James 1:5-7). Jesus did say, "Ask and ye shall receive" (Matthew 7:7).

Wisdom will save you from evil people (2:12) and the immoral woman (2:16). It will keep you out of trouble (7:15) and extend your life. Having wisdom is the functional equivalent of having riches and honor (8:18).

Thought for Proverbs 3:16

If you need it, then ask for it. "If any of you lack wisdom, let him ask of God, that giveth to all men liberally, and upbraided not; and it shall be given him" (James 1:5).

Discussion Questions for Proverbs 3:16

1. What is a proverb?

2. What is wisdom?

3. Who is the wisdom of God?

4. What does it mean to "get an understanding?"

"Moreover, I saw here under the sun that, where justice ought to be, there was wickedness; and where righteousness ought to be, there was wickedness."

(Ecclesiastes 3:16, The Revised English Bible)

Introduction to Ecclesiastes 3:16

Life is full of seasons, and each season has its own challenges. For instance, there is a time to be born, to die, to plant, to pluck up, to kill, to heal, to break down, to buildup, and to weep. There is a time to laugh, to mourn, to dance, to cast away stones, to gather stones, to embrace, to refrain from embracing, to get, to lose, and to keep. There is a time to cast away, to rend, to sew, to keep silent, to speak, to love, to hate, to [make] war, and for peace (3:1-8). As the wisest man in the then-known world, Solomon saw a little bit of everything!

Examination of Ecclesiastes 3:16

As I read this passage, it reminded me of what some people say about our criminal justice system. "Some people get away with murder because they have money." To use Deacon Henry James Patterson words, **"You may get by, but you won't get away!"** God is watching us, as "all things are naked and opened unto the eyes of him with whom we have to do" (Hebrews 4:13).

A nation's leaders should not take brides (Exodus 23:8; Deuteronomy 16:18-19) or favor one group over another (Exodus 23:3). The scripture declares, "He that ruleth over men must rule just, ruling in the fear of God" (2nd Samuel 23:2).

The prophet Isaiah declared, "Woe unto them that call evil good, and good evil: that put darkness for light, and light for darkness; that put bitter for sweet, and sweet for bitter" (5:20). If we love the Lord, we would not be guilty of this.

Jesus said, "…men loved darkness rather than light, because their deeds were evil" (John 3:19).

Thought for Ecclesiastes 3:16

Preaching is good, but living what you preach is better. "Righteousness exalted a nation: but sin is a reproach to any people" (Proverbs 14:34).

Discussion Questions for Ecclesiastes 3:16

1. What is justice?

2. What is righteousness?

3. What is wickedness?

4. Which season are you in?

"Moreover the Lord saith, Because the daughters of Zion are haughty, and walk with stretched forth necks and wanton eyes, walking and mincing as they go, and making a tinkling with their feet."

(Isaiah 3:16)

Introduction to Isaiah 3:16

Isaiah is one of three "major" prophets, and the book of Isaiah is the longest book in the Bible. Isaiah was the son of Amoz, he lived in Jerusalem (7:1-3), was married (8:3), and had two sons (7:3; 8:3). In the book of Isaiah, Jesus is called the Branch (10:1), the root of Jesse (10:1, 10), and God's elect and servant (42:1). According to Smith (2002), "Isaiah is a collection of sermons and prophesies."

When God called him (6), Isaiah said, "Here am I; send

me" (6:8). Isaiah was a southern kingdom prophet, who ministered during the reigns of Uzziah, Jotham, Ahaz, and Hezekiah. God showed Isaiah a vision concerning Judah and Jerusalem (1:1).

Jesus quoted from Isaiah. In Mark 7:6-8, Jesus called the Pharisees hypocrites and used Isaiah's prophesy as proof (Isaiah 29:13). One day Jesus went into the synagogue (Luke 4:16-19) and read Isaiah 61:1-3. When Jesus told the twelve that the son of man must suffer, be rejected, and killed (Mark 8:31), he quoted Isaiah 50:6; 53. When Jesus said, "My house shall be called the house of prayer" (Matthew 21:13), he quoted Isaiah 56:7.

Examination of Isaiah 3:16

Isaiah prophesied against the house of Judah because she sinned openly before the Lord (3:8-9). Chapter 3:1-15 highlights the suffering and captivity that lied ahead for Judah because of her sins (3:8-7). The righteous were spared but the wicked reaped what she had sown (3:10-11).

The Lord was not pleased with the leadership because they took advantage of the people (3:13-14). The Lord rebuked them when he said, "How dare you crush people and grind the faces of the poor" (3:15, Tanakh).

Moreover, the Lord was not pleased with the daughters of Zion, as she was arrogant ("haughty") and wanted everything that she saw ("wanton eyes"). Not only was she haughty, she was loud and wanted to be seen by all. The daughters of Zion "loved the world" (1st John 2:15-17).

Thought for Isaiah 3:16

Is the Lord pleased with you? "When a man's ways please the LORD, he maketh even his enemies to be at peace with him"

(Proverbs 16:7). Is the Lord pleased with you?

Discussion Questions for Isaiah 3:16

1. Who were the daughters of Zion?

2. Define mince.

3. How did Judah sin?

"And it shall come to pass, when ye shall be multiplied and increased in the land, in those days, saith the Lord, they shall say no more, The ark of the covenant of the Lord: neither shall it come to mind: neither shall they remember it; neither shall they visit it; neither shall that be done any more."

(Jeremiah 3:16)

Introduction to Jeremiah 3:16

Jeremiah is the second longest book in the Bible with 52 chapters. He was a southern kingdom prophet from the tribe of Benjamin. As far as we know, Jeremiah was not married (16:1).

God called and sanctified him before he was born (1:5). God told Jeremiah, "Go where I send you, say what I tell you to say, and do not be afraid of the people's face" (1:7, Tanakh). God told Jeremiah, "I am with you, and I will deliver you" (1:8).

His mission was to "to uproot and to pull down, to destroy and to overthrow, to build and to plant" (1:10, Tanakh). Due to the nature of his ministry, Jeremiah was scourged and cast into prison (20:1-3; 37:15-18). Some of the princes [of the people] hated and wanted to kill him (38:1-6). No matter what he suffered, Jeremiah was obedient and spoke for the Lord.

Examination of Jeremiah 3:16

Built into the text is a promise (prophesy) of prosperity and, in a sense, longevity. This [text] appears to be a message of hope. If Israel repented, she would multiply, increase in the land, be fertile, and [would subsequently] stop asking about, thinking about, and talking about the Ark of the Covenant.

Israel and Judah backslide by falling into apostasy (2:5). God asked Israel and Judah, "What wrong did your fathers find in me" (2:5)? Although Israel and Judah played the harlot (2:20), the Lord still wanted her back (3:2).

Israel, however, would not repent. Because of her lifestyle, God gave her a bill of divorcement and put her away (3:8). Judah acted as if she wanted to repent but did not mean it. "Judah hath not returned unto me with her whole heart but feignedly" (3:10).

Israel tried to justify herself more than her treacherous sister Judah (3:11). The Lord told Israel, "Return to me. If you do, I will not cause mine angry to fall upon you; for I am merciful" (3:12-14). God told Jeremiah to tell backsliding Israel, "Turn; for I am married to you (3:14). If Israel turned back to God, he would give her pastors after his own heart (3:15).

Thought for Jeremiah 3:16

Repent and seek the Lord. "Seek ye the LORD while he may be found, call ye upon him while he is near" (Isaiah 55:6).

Discussion Questions for Jeremiah 3:16

1. What is a bill of divorcement?

2. What does it mean to repent?

3. What does the Bible say about anger?

4. What was in the Ark of the Covenant?

5. How did the word of the Lord come to Jeremiah?

6. What did God mean by "for I am merciful" (v.12)?

7. How did Israel and Judah backslide?

"He hath also broken my teeth with gravel stones, he hath covered me with ashes."

(Lamentations 3:16)

Introduction to Lamentations 3:16

Lamentations is a short book of "poetry" with five chapters and 154 verses. It is believed that the prophet Jeremiah wrote it, but we have no biblical-proof (evidence) that he did. Whoever wrote Lamentations, no doubt, saw what had happened in Zion. In our Protestant Bible, the book of Lamentations is sandwiched in between Jeremiah and Ezekiel.

You never miss your water until your well runs dry! Judah learned this the hard way! In 586 B.C., Nebuchadnezzar besieged, plundered, burned, and destroyed the "city of the great king" (Matthew 5:35). Nebuchadnezzar took Judah into captivity because of her sins (1st Chronicles 9:1). No matter how God tried to correct her, she ignored him (Isaiah 65:25).

Lamenting, weeping, or crying is a human response. For instance, Esau wept when he did not get his father's blessing (Genesis 27:1-38). Esau and Jacob wept when they were reunited (Genesis 33:1-4). When Jacob was told that Joseph was dead, he cried (Genesis 37:25-35). Joseph wept when he saw his brothers (Genesis 45:1-4), Israel wept when Moses died (Deuteronomy 34:7-8), and Hannah wept because she was tired of being picked on and childless (1st Samuel 1:7, 10).

Samuel wept when God rejected Saul (1ˢᵗ Samuel 16:1-2), Judah wept when she remembered Zion (Psalm 137:1), and Peter wept when the cock crowed (Luke 22:62). Moreover, Y'Shua (Jesus) wept over Jerusalem and Lazarus (Luke 19:41; John11:41). The messianic community wept over Stephen (Acts 7-8:2), and as believers, we cry too. The Lord, however, helps us to move on!

Examination of Lamentations 3:16

The prophet said that God broke his teeth with gravel stones but did not say "how" or "why" he did it. The prophet declared, "He covered me with ashes." Why did God cover him (Jeremiah) with ashes?

Thought for Lamentations 3:16

Weeping may cleanse your soul. "They that sow in tears shall reap in joy" (Psalm 126:5).

Discussion Questions for Lamentations 3:16

1. What are gravel stones?

2. What does the Bible say about a broken tooth?

3. Why would the Lord cover someone with ashes?

"And it came to pass at the end of seven days, that the word of the LORD came unto me, saying."

(Ezekiel 3:16)

Introduction to Ezekiel 3:16

Ezekiel is the third "major" prophet and the fourth largest book in the Bible. Ezekiel was a Levite (1:3), a priest (1:3), the son of Buzi (1:3), and a descendant of Zadok. He was married (24:15-18) but did not have any children (supposedly).

Ezekiel was taken into exile by king Nebuchadnezzar. While in exile, he preached to Judah, but she would not listen. A note in the **Original African Heritage Bible** says that "Ezekiel was the only priest to prophesy outside of Jerusalem other than Jeremiah".

God called, prepared, and sent Ezekiel to the house of Israel (2:3; 3:4). God said, "Son of man, I send thee to the children of Israel, to a rebellious nation that hath rebelled against me: they and their fathers have transgressed against me, even unto this very day" (2:3). Moreover, God said, "Do not fear them and do not fear their words (2:6, Tanakh), but speak My words to them, whether they listen or not, for they are rebellious" (2:7, Tanakh). God told Ezekiel that Israel was a "nation of rebels" (2:3, Tanakh) and a "rebellious breed" (2:5, 8: 3:9, Tanakh).

Examination of Ezekiel 3:16

Ezekiel was translated like Philip and taken to Telabib (3:14; Acts 8:39-40). While there, Ezekiel sat with his brother (who was in captivity) for seven days and marveled at what he saw. On the eighth day, the Lord spoke to Ezekiel and said, "Son of man, I have made thee a watchman unto the house of Israel: therefore hear the word at my mouth, and give them warning from me" (3:17).

God used Ezekiel in hopes of delivering his people. His job was "to cry loud and spare not" (Isaiah 58:1). God told him to warn his people. If Ezekiel obeyed God and warned Israel, he would deliver his soul (3:19). If he was disobedient ("failed to warn Israel") and she died in her sins, Israel's blood would be on his hands (3:20).

Thought for Ezekiel 3:16

Speak as you are moved by the Holy Ghost. "For the prophecy came not in old time by the will of man: but holy men of God spake as they were moved by the Holy Ghost" (2nd Peter 1:20).

Discussion Questions for Ezekiel 3:16

1. How did the word of the Lord come to Ezekiel?

2. What happened on the 7th day?

3. What is a vision?

4. Where is Telabib?

"Shadrach, Meshach, and Abed-nego, answered and said to the king, O Nebuchadnezzar, we are not careful to answer thee in this matter."

(Daniel 3:16)

Introduction to Daniel 3:16

It is believed that the Book of Daniel (BoD) was written between 540 and 530 B.C. Y'Shua (Jesus) was familiar with the BoD and called him a prophet (Matthew 24:15).

When Nebuchadnezzar took Judah into captivity, Jehoiakim was her king. When Judah arrived in Babylon, Nebuchadnezzar took the "cream of the crop" and socialized (trained) them in the ways of the Chaldeans (1:4). Daniel and the three Hebrew boys were selected but [they] would not eat or drink anything from the king's table.

One night, Nebuchadnezzar had a dream that troubled his soul. When he woke up, he could not remember it. Therefore, he summoned the wise men and ordered them to recall and interpret his dream. When they could not recall let alone interpret his dream, he flew into a rage. In his anger, he decreed that all of the wise men in Babylon be put to death.

When news of the decree came to Daniel's ear, he prayed. The Lord heard him (Psalm 34:15) and gave him the ability (wisdom) to recall and interpret the king's dream. As such, none of the wise men died.

In regards to dreams, God used dreams to direct the wise men (Matthew 2:12) and Joseph (Matthew 1:18-25; 2:13-15; 2:19-21). God used dreams to show Joseph things to come (Genesis 37:5-8, 9-13) and to help others (Genesis 40-41). Joseph was called a "dreamer" (Genesis 37:19). In our age, God uses dreams to get our attention (Job 33:14-17). Dreams are a part of the human experience, as the prophet Joel declared, "...your old men shall dream dreams" (2:28).

In Daniel chapter 2, Nebuchadnezzar "acted" on the dream and had a golden image built: he made his subjects, under the threat of death, bow down and worship it (3:1-7). Because Shadrach, Meshach, and Abednego were faithful to the God of Abraham, Isaac, and Jacob, they ignored the decree (3).

One day, [some of] the Chaldeans told Nebuchadnezzar that Shadrach, Meshach, and Abednego ignored the decree and did not serve his gods or bow down to the golden image. In a fit of rage, Nebuchadnezzar summed the three Hebrew boys and confronted them. "Is it true? You do not serve my gods nor worship the golden image [of me]?" He gave them an ultimatum—Bow down and worship the golden image or die!

Examination of Daniel 3:16

The Hebrew boys were in the hot seat but were "swift to hear, slow to speak, and slow to wrath" (James 1:19). With grace and humility, Shadrach, Meshach, and Abednego said, "If it be so, our God whom we serve is able to deliver us from the burning fiery furnace, and he will deliver us out of thine hand, O king. But if not, be it known unto thee, O king, that we will not serve thy gods, nor worship the golden image which thou has set up" (3:17-18). The king flew into a rage and threw them into a fiery furnace.

Thought for Daniel 3:16

You can do it with Jesus. "Thou therefore endure hardness, as a good solider of Jesus Christ" (2nd Timothy 2:3).

Discussion Questions for Daniel 3:16

1. What is a fiery trial?

2. How tall was the golden image?

3. What was Daniel's Hebrew name?

4. Who were the wise men?

"The LORD also shall roar out of Zion, and utter his voice from Jerusalem; and the heavens and the earth shall shake: but the LORD will be the hope of his people, and the strength of the children of Israel."

(Joel 3:16)

Introduction to Joel 3:16

Joel is one of twelve short prophetic books in the Hebrew Bible. According to Carmody, Carmody, and Cohen (1988), the number 12 is [allegedly] symbolic of the twelve tribes of Israel.

Joel is the second book among the "minor" prophets. It has three chapters and 73 verses. Joel's name means "the Lord is God." Joel was a southern kingdom prophet, who lived during the reign of Uzziah (Matthew, 1978).

The apostle Peter used Joel's prophesy to explain what happened when the 120 received the gift of the Holy Ghost on the day of Pentecost (Acts 2:1-4). In light of the move of God, the people (multitude) were confounded and assumed that the 120 were "full of new wine" (Acts 2:5-13). Peter said, "These are not drunken as ye suppose, seeing that it is but the ninth hour. But this is that which was spoken by the prophet Joel" (Joel 2:28-32; Acts 2:15-21).

Examination of Joel 3:16

The Lord will fight for and redeem his people. God wanted Judah to repent, fast, pray, and weep before him (2:12-14). Moreover, God wanted the priests and ministers to call a solemn assembly, to cry out to him, and plead for the people (2:15-17). In turn, God would answer her (Israel's) prayers, restore what the locusts had destroyed, give her plenty of food, and then make his presence known.

In regards to locusts, God used locusts to humble the Egyptians (Exodus 10), as locusts were one of the ten plagues. In this passage, God used locusts to punish (humble) Judah (Deuteronomy 28:38, 42).

When Israel was in the wilderness, she ate locusts (Leviticus 11:21-22). Moreover, John the Baptist ate them (Matthew 3:3; Mark 1:6). The scripture declares, "The locusts have no king, yet go they forth all of them by band" (Proverbs 30:27).

Thought for Joel 3:16

The Lord is alive and well. "The LORD liveth; and blessed be my rock; and let the God of my salvation be exalted" (Psalm 18:46).

Discussion Questions for Joel 3:16

1. What is a locust?

2. What is the valley of Jehoshaphat?

3. What is Pentecost?

"Thou hast multiplied they merchants above the stars of heaven: the cankerworm spoileth, and flieth away."

(Nahum 3:16)

Introduction to Nahum 3:16

Nahum is one of the 12 "minor" prophets. The book of Nahum has three chapters and forty-seven verses. The prophet highlights the destruction, doom, or fall of Ninevah (Halley, 1965).

Nahum was the second prophet that God sent to Ninevah. In 785 B.C., God sent Jonah (Halley, 1965), and Ninevah repented at the preaching of Jonah (Jonah 3:1-10; Matthew 12:41). About 150 years later, God sent the prophet Nahum to rebuke her (Halley, 1965). Nahum was a southern kingdom prophet.

Ninevah was the capital city of the Assyrian Empire (Halley, 1965). It was founded by Nimrod, who was a mighty hunter before the Lord (Genesis 10:8-9).

The prophet Zephaniah cried out against Ninevah, "And

he will stretch out his hand against the North, and destroy Assyria; and will make Ninevah a desolation, and dry like a wilderness" (Zephaniah 2:13). The Assyrians were high-minded (Zephaniah 2:15). "This is the rejoicing city that dwelt carelessly, that said in her heart, I am, and there is none beside me."

The phrases "I am" and "there is none beside me" should ring a bell in your mind. God (YHVH) told Moses to tell the children of Israel, "I AM hath sent thee" (Exodus 3:13-15). Messiah said, "Before Abraham was, I am" (John 8:58). YHVH said through Isaiah, "I am the Lord, and there is none else, there is no God beside me" (Isaiah 44:6; 45:5, 6, 18, and 22; 46:9). Perhaps, the people of Ninevah were familiar with Hebrew scripture and tried to use them to slam Israel and Judah!

Nahum (1: 1-7) lists some of the attributes of God (YHVH). YHVH is jealous (Exodus 20:5), vengeful (Deuteronomy 32:35; Psalm 94:1; Romans 12:19), and furious (Ezekiel 5:15). He (YHVH) is slow to anger (Psalm 103:8; 145:8; Joel 2:13), good (Psalm 34:8), and all-knowing (Psalm 8:4; Proverbs 15:3).

Examination of Nahum 3:16

Once again, Ninevah caught God's eye, and he was not pleased with Ninevah. "I am against thee, and I will show the nations thy nakedness, and the kingdoms thy shame" (3:5). Moreover, "I will cast abominable filth upon thee, and make thee the vile, and will set thee as a gazing stock" (3:6). To say the least, God was not pleased with her.

Thought for Nahum 3:16

To use the words of Deacon Henry James Patterson, "You

may get by, but you won't get away". "The face of the Lord is against them that do evil, to cut off the remembrance of them from the earth" (Psalm 34:16).

Discussion Questions for Nahum 3:16

1. What is a cankerworm?

2. Define high minded.

3. How did Ninevah respond to Nahum's message?

4. Which tribe was Nahum from?

"When I heard, my belly trembled; my lips quivered at the voice: rottenness entered into my bones, and I trembled in myself, that I might rest in the day of trouble: when he cometh up unto the people, he will invade them with his troops."

(Habakkuk 3:16)

Introduction to Habakkuk 3:16

The Book of Habakkuk is one of the 12 "minor" prophets, with three chapters and fifty-six verses. In his work, the prophet told the world that the Lord is from everlasting (1:12) and is in his holy temple (2:20).

Habakkuk felt that the Lord was not listening to him. God showed him a vision of how he was going to raise up the Chaldeans to chastise and correct Judah. After the Chaldeans chastised Judah, God destroyed them. God told Habakkak, "Write the vision, and make it plain upon tables that they may run that readeth it."

Examination of Habakkuk 3:16

This verse is a part of Habakkuk's prayer. God marched through the land and walked through the sea with his horses. When Habakkuk heard the sound of the Lord marching and walking, it scared him.

Thought for Habakkuk 3:16

Correction is good for you. "Behold, happy is the man whom God correcteth: therefore despise not thou the chastening of the Almighty" (Job 5:17).

Discussion Questions for Habakkuk 3:16

1. Who were the Chaldeans?

2. What is a burden?

3. What does the text mean by tremble?

"In that day it shall be said to Jerusalem, Fear thou not: and to Zion, Let not thine hands be slack."

(Zephaniah 3:16)

Introduction to Zephaniah 3:16

The Book of Zephaniah is a short book, with three chapters and fifty-three verses. Zephaniah lived in Jerusalem during the reign of Josiah (1st Kings 22:1; 2nd Chronicles 34:1) and was a southern kingdom prophet. Zephaniah prophesied fifty years after the death of Isaiah (Birnbaum, 1998).

Examination of Zephaniah 3:16

This is a prophecy of hope. Although God was going to judge the southern kingdom (Judah), he did not want her to give up.

Thought for Zephaniah 3:16

God has feelings. "His angry endureth but a moment. In his favor is life. Weeping may endure for a night but joy cometh in the morning" (Psalm 30:5).

Discussion Questions for Zephaniah 3:16

1. How many people are called Zephaniah in scripture?

2. Who should we fear?

3. What does slack mean?

"Then they that feared the LORD spake often one to another: and the LORD hearkened, and heard it, and a book of remembrance was written before him for them that feared the LORD, and that thought upon his name."

(Malachi 3:16)

Introduction to Malachi 3:16

Malachi is the last "minor" prophet. He prophesied during the ministry of Nehemiah (Matthew, 1978) and is [called] the last Old Testament prophet (Halley, 1965; Unger, 1966).

We learn from Malachi that God loved Jacob (Israel) and hated Esau (1:2). Although he loved Israel, she did not honor nor respect him (1:6-13). Because his people were brazen, they (Israel) wearied the Lord with their [empty] words (2:17).

Malachi chapter 3 is "famous" for its teaching on tithing. Under Torah, the eleven tribes of Israel and (perhaps) proselytes to Judaism gave a tenth to Levi as a means of support (Hebrews 7:1-9). Under grace and truth, tithing is NOT compulsory (Acts 15), as Jews and gentiles, who accept Y'Shua as Messiah, should willingly give what the Lord tells him or her to give and/or whatever he or she purposes in his or her heart (2ⁿᵈ Corinthians 9:7). Thus a person in Christ should give willingly and freely from the heart, without fear of contradiction. According to Torah, God told Moses to tell the children of Israel to tithe, not the Holy Ghost church.

Examination of Malachi 3:16

This verse demonstrates that God listens to and respond to what we say.

Thought for Malachi 3:16

Where is the Lord? "The Lord is in his holy temple: let all the earth keep silence before him" (Habakkuk 2:20).

Discussion Questions on Malachi 3:16

1. What was the storehouse?

2. What were the spoils of war?

3. Why did Abraham tithe?

THE MESSIANIC SCRIPTURES
(The New Testament)

THE GOSPELS

"Immediately when he came up from the water, the heavens were opened to him and he saw the Spirit of God coming down like a dove, and it dwelt upon him."

(Matthew 3:16, Hebrew Gospel of Matthew)

About Matthew

Before Matthew became a disciple and an apostle, he was a publican (10:3). As an ambassador for Messiah, Jesus gave him power to heal the sick (Matthew 10:1), cast out devils (Mark 3:15; 6:12-13), and to bind and loose on earth (Matthew 18:18). Matthew was present at the last supper (26) and spent forty days with Jesus after his passion (Acts 1:3). He saw Jesus and Peter walk on water (14:23-29) and Jesus taken up (Acts 1:9).

Along with the other apostles, Jesus told Matthew not to leave Jerusalem (Luke 24:49) but to wait for the promise of the Father (Acts 1:4). Because he obeyed the Lord and tarried in Jerusalem, he received the gift of the Holy Ghost (Acts 2:1-4), spoke in tongues, and supported Peter when he preached on Pentecost (Acts 2:14-47).

Matthew was active in the mother church (Acts 6); he was courageous (Acts 8:1) and present at the first church council (Acts 15). His name is cited four times in the gospels (9:9; 10:3; Mark 3:18; Luke 6:15).

Introduction to Matthew 3:16

The gospel of Matthew is associated with the apostle Matthew, as tradition holds that he wrote it. However, we have no biblical-proof that he did. Of the four gospels, Matthew' is the longest with twenty-eight chapters.

All of the synoptic gospels, Matthew (3:13-17), Mark (1:9-11) and Luke (3:21-22), record the baptism of Jesus. Each account, however, is slightly different but conveys the same message—Jesus was baptized!

According to the synoptic gospels, John baptized the common people and Jesus in the Jordan. They received John's baptism (Luke 9:29), but the Pharisees and lawyers rejected it (Luke 9:30). When the common people came for baptism, they confessed their sins (Matthew 3:5-6; Mark 1:5). Unlike them, Jesus did not have any sins to confess (Hebrews 4:15). Jesus was (and still is!) blameless and without blemish (1st Peter 1:19).

When Jesus came to John to get baptized, he (John) protested and said, "I have need to be baptized of thee" (3:13-14). Nonetheless, Jesus did not yield to John's protest but simply said, "Suffer it to be so" (Matthew 3:15). Thus, out of obedience, John baptized Jesus "in order to fulfill all righteousness" (3:15), not for the remission of sins (Acts 2:38). John's baptism was unto repentance (Matthew 3:11) and was a break from self-immersion. According to the Hebrew writer, baptism is one of the "principles of the doctrine of Christ" (Hebrews 6:1-2).

John the Baptist was the first person, as far as we know, in the history of the world to baptize others (Stegemann, 1998), followed by the twelve (apostles). The twelve baptized under Jesus' watchful eye (John 3:22; 4:1-2) and after his ascension (Acts 2:38). According to the Acts of the Apostles, Philip, who was one of the seven (6:1-6) and an evangelist (21:8), baptized the Samaritans (8:12-16) and the Ethiopian eunuch (8:26-39). Anaias baptized Brother Saul (9:17-18), whereas Peter baptized the house of Cornelius (10:44-48). The apostle Paul baptized Lydia and her household (16:14-15), the prison keeper and his family (16:27-33), and twelve certain disciples (19-1-7): he (Paul) also baptized Crispus, Gaius, and the household of Stephanas (1st Corinthians 1:14-17). Jesus, however, did not baptize anyone in water. As he declared, "For John truly baptized with water; but ye shall be baptized [by me] with the Holy Ghost not many days hence "(Acts 1:5).

Examination of Matthew 3:16

As noted, Jesus was baptized in the Jordan "to fulfill all righteous" (Matthew 3:15), not for the remission of sins (Acts 2:38). The gospel of John seems to suggest that John the Baptist (the Baptist) did not know what Jesus looked like. According to the gospel of John, God told the Baptist, "The one on whom you will see the Spirit coming down and resting is the man who baptizes with the Holy Spirit" (1:33, The New Testament in Modern English). God used the sign of the dove to let the Baptist know who Jesus was. According to Matthew 3:17, Mark 1:11, and Luke 3:22, a voice from heaven said, "This is my beloved son in whom I am well pleased."

The Jordan has its place in the sun. Under Joshua's leadership, the children of Israel walked through the Jordan in order to go into the promise land (Joshua 3:9-17). Naaman dipped himself in the Jordan River seven times and was healed from leprosy (2nd Kings 5:1-14), and Jesus was baptized in the Jordan River.

Thought for Matthew 3:16

John baptized Jesus, but who baptized you? "Repent, and be baptized every one of you in the name of Jesus Christ for the remission of sins, and ye shall receive the gift of the Holy Ghost" (Acts 2:38).

Discussion Questions for Matthew 3:16

1. Who was older, Y'Shua (Jesus) or John the Baptist?

2. How old was Y'Shua when he got baptized?

3. Was Matthew a republican?

4. Was Matthew called by any other name?

"There was Simon, whom he surnamed Peter."

(Mark 3:16, The Bible: A New Translation)

About Peter

By trade, Peter was a fisherman (Matthew 4:18). He was married, a disciple (Matthew 19:1-4), one of the twelve, and [a] part of Jesus' inner circle (Matthew 8:14, 10:1-4; 17:1-9). Peter saw Jesus transfigured (Mark 9:2-9 and Luke 8:41-42, 51-56) and walk on water (Matthew 14:25, Mark 6:48, and John 6:18). Peter had a brother who was a disciple and an apostle (Matthew 19:1-4).

Jesus gave Peter power (authority) to heal the sick, cast out demons, and to bind and loose in heaven and on earth (3:1; Matthew 16:19). Jesus also promised to give him the keys to the kingdom (Matthew 16:19).

Peter rebuked Jesus (Matthew 16:21-33; Mark 8:33). Then, Jesus turned around and rebuked him. Out of pure love and compassion for him, Jesus prayed that the devil would not sift Peter like wheat (Luke 22:31-32). Jesus prophesied that Peter would deny him (Matthew 26:33-35; Mark 14:29-31; Luke 22:33-34). Although he said that he would not do it, Peter denied Jesus three times (Matthew 26:69-75; Mark 14:66-72; Luke 22:54-62).

Peter received the gift of the Holy Ghost (Acts 2:1-4) and was the key note speaker on Pentecost (Acts 2:11-40). God used him to convert the house of Cornelius (Acts 10, 11) and as a spokesman in the first church council (Acts 15:7-11). As far as we know, Peter was the only apostle who walked on water (Matthew 14:22-33). Two epistles bear his name: 1st and 2nd Peter.

Introduction to Mark 3:16

According to the late Dr. James Strong, to surname means "to address [someone] by an additional title, to entitle, or to call." The term "surname" can be found in the book of Isaiah. "One shall say, I am the LORD's; and another shall call himself by the name Jacob; and another shall subscribe with his hand unto the LORD, and surname himself by the name of Israel" (Isaiah 44:5). In another place it says, "For Jacob's my servant's sake, and Israel mine elect, I have called thee by thy name: I have surnamed thee, though thou has not known me" (Isaiah 45:4).

Examination of Mark 3:16

Jesus surnamed (called) Simon Peter. Mark 3:17 says that he surnamed James and John "Boanerges", which is, the sons of thunder. Judas was surnamed Iscariot (Luke 22:3), and Joseph was called Barnabas was surnamed Justus (Acts 1:23). Joses was surnamed Barnabus by the apostles (Acts 4:36), whereas God changed Abram to Abraham (Genesis 17:5), Sarai to Sarah (Genesis 17:15), and Jacob to Israel (Genesis 32:28).

We may think that God changed Sha'ul's (Saul's) name to Paul, but we have no biblical-proof for this. According to what we know, God did not tell Sha'ul that "thy name shall be called Paul." When God blinded "Paul" on his way to Damascus, he called him Sha'ul (Acts 9:4; 22:7; 26:14). God sent Ananias to Sha'ul (Acts 9:10-11), not Paul. Ananias called him, "Brother Sha'ul" (Acts 22:13). Barnabas found Sha'ul in Tarsus (Acts 11:25). Moreover, Acts 12:25 says that "Barnabas and Sha'ul returned from Jerusalem."

With the exception of Stern (The Jewish New Testament) and The Institute for Scripture Research (The Scriptures), all of our English translations call Sha'ul Paul. The late Dr. James Strong noted in his exhaustive concordance that "Saul" (Sha'ul) is the Jewish name of Paul.

When Sha'ul's name was (allegedly) changed to Paul is a mystery. One source said that Sha'ul is the original name of Paul, and that he changed it to Paul (Murphy 1989, p. 318 and 417). Perhaps, Paul was Sha'ul' cognomen (Cognomen-Wikipedia, the free encyclopedia; Bruce, 1977)?

Thought for Mark 3:16

What are you called? "Then said Thomas, which is called Didymus, unto his fellow disciples, Let us also go, that we may die with him" (John 11:16).

Discussion Questions for Mark 3:16

1. Who was Mark?

2. Was Mark a disciple or an apostle of Jesus Christ?

3. What is a disciple?

4. What is an apostle?

"John answered, saying unto them all, I indeed baptize you with water; but one mightier than I cometh, the latchet of whose shoes I am not worthy to unloose: he shall baptize you with the Holy Ghost and with fire."

(Luke 3:16)

Introduction to Luke 3:16

It is believed that Dr. Luke wrote the gospel of Luke and the Acts of the Apostles, but we have no biblical-proof for it. Luke wrote to Theophilus, who was a high ranking Roman official (1:3). According to the gospel of Luke, he used eyewitness testimonies and his knowledge of events to write his work. Luke's name is mentioned three times in the New Testament: Colossians 4:11, Philemon 24, and 2nd Timothy 4:11.

The gospel of Luke is the 2nd largest gospel with 24 chapters. Luke, the physician, was not an apostle. Instead, he was a companion of Paul (2nd Timothy 4:11). When all men forsook Paul, Dr. Luke supported him (2nd Timothy 4).

About John the Baptist

John the Baptist was "the voice of one crying in the wilderness" (Isaiah 40:3): he was the Lord's messenger (Malachi 3:1) and a prophet (9:24-29). Because John was a prophet, it is reasonable to assume that he had a gift of discernment (1st Corinthians 12:10).

John preached the baptism of repentance for the remission of sins (Mark 1:4; 3:3), had disciples (5:33), and was a great man (1:15). Moreover, the common people respected him and wanted to hear what he had to say (3:11-14). Some people, however, hated him (Matthew 14:1-5; 12-13; John 6:4).

John the Baptist was from the tribe of Levi (1:5), his father was a priest (1:5-9), and his parents had him in their old age (1:13, 18; 2:57). According to the covenant of circumcision (Genesis 17:9-14), John was circumcised on the eight day (Luke 1:59). Indeed, he was the Elijah of prophecy (Malachi 4:5-6; Luke 1:5-25; 2:57-80).

John the Baptist was a Nazarite (Numbers 6). For food, he ate locust and wild honey (Leviticus 11:22; Matthew 3:4). John lived in the desert (Luke 1:80), preached in the Lower Jordan (Halley, 1965), and, as noted, baptized the common people and Jesus. John the Baptist received the gift of the Holy Ghost in his mother's womb (Luke 1:15).

Examination of Luke 3:16

The people wanted to know if John the Baptist were the Messiah (3:15). John told them that he was NOT the Messiah, "the coming one," or "desire of all nations." In this passage, John made a distinction between himself and Messiah (Christ).

Thought for Luke 3:16

Humility carries the day. "Humble yourselves therefore under the mighty hand of God, that he may exalt you in due time" (1st Peter 5:6).

Discussion Questions for Luke 3:16

1. How long did John the Baptist preach the word?

2. How did he die?

3. What did Jesus say about him?

4. What is repentance?

"For God so loved the world, that he gave his only begotten Son, that whosoever believeth in him should not perish, but have everlasting life."

(John 3:16)

About the apostle John

It is church tradition that the apostle John wrote the gospel of John, 1st, 2nd, and 3rd John, and the book of Revelation. We do not know the name of his tribe, who his mother was, or where he was born and raised. We do know, however, that John was one of the sons of Zebedee and that James was his brother (Matthew 10:1-4).

The apostle John was at the transfiguration and was a part of Jesus' inner circle (Mark 9:2-8; Luke 9:28-36). John was with Jesus in the garden (Matthew 26:37; Mark 14:33; Luke 22:39), he stood in the crowd during Jesus' trial (John 18), and saw him crucified (John 19). No doubt, Jesus trusted him as he [Jesus] left his mother in his care (John 19:26).

Our precious brother was present when Jesus appeared to the eleven (Matthew 28:16). He spent forty days with Jesus after his passion (Acts 1:3) and saw him ascend into heaven (Mark 16:19; Acts 1:9-11). John received the gift of the Holy Ghost (Acts 2:4) and was locked up and beaten for preaching the word (Acts 4, 5). John was a traveling evangelist (Acts 8:14-17) and a pillar in the church (Galatians 2:9). He was present at the first church council in Jerusalem (Acts 15).

Introduction to John 3:16

Nicodemus started a conversion with Jesus but did not get a chance to finish it. The Bible does not tell us "why" Nicodemus went to Jesus by night or what he wanted to talk about. Perhaps, Nicodemus wanted to talk with Jesus about the miracles that he had performed? The text seems to suggest that Jesus cut him off and said, "Except a man be born again, he cannot see the kingdom of heaven" (3:3).

As a Jewish rabbi, Pharisee, and member of the Sanhedrin (3:1), Nicodemus was probably taken aback by Jesus' words. In turn, he asked two questions (3:4, 9). Jesus listened, answered Nicodemus's questions, and marveled at his carnality.

Examination of John 3:16

Jesus told Nicodemus that God loved the world and gave his only begotten son. Jesus is begotten in that he is unique and one of a kind. There is no one on earth or in heaven like him, as Jesus cannot be imitated or duplicated! Moreover, as a function of God's love, he sent his son (Jesus) into the world to take away our sins (John 1:29).

In this text, we see love in action. There were no strings attached to God's love for the human family because he loved the world "in deed and in truth" (1st John 3:18). In regards to God's love, we cannot barter, borrow, buy, hide, sell, snatch, or steal it.

Jesus said that "whosoever believeth in him should not perish". This means that our faith must be in Jesus alone. As the scripture declares, "Whosoever will, let him come" (Revelation

22:17). Whosever will is an open invitation to ALL.

Thought for John 3:16

Are you one of God's sons? "Beloved, now are we the sons of God, and it doth not yet appear what we shall be: but we know that, when he shall appear, we shall be like him; for we shall see him as he is" (1st John 3:2). If you are in Christ, then you are one of God's sons or daughters (see 2nd Corinthians 6:16-18).

Discussion Questions for John 3:16

1. Who wrote the gospel of John?

2. What is love?

3. Who were the Pharisees?

4. Define begotten?

THE ACTS OF THE APOSTLES

"And his name through faith in his name hath made this man strong, whom ye see and know: yea, the faith which is by him hath given him this perfect soundness in the presence of you all."

(Acts 3:16)

Introduction to Acts 3:16

Jesus "healed" people who were oppressed by the devil (10:38) and was criticized for healing them (Matthew 21:14-15; 21:23). Now, the apostles were being questioned and attacked for healing someone.

Healing someone was not new to Peter or John. When Jesus sent out the 12 (Matthew 10:1, 8; Mark 6:12-12) and the seventy (Luke 10:1-9), they healed people under his supervision (watchful eye). When God used Peter and John to heal the lame man, Jesus was in heavenly places (Mark 16:19; Acts 7:56).

This text does not say that Peter and John laid [their] hands on the lame man (Mark 16:17-18). Moreover, this text does not say that Peter and John prayed over him and anointed him with oil in the name of the Lord (James 5:14). Like Jesus (Matthew 8:8-13; Luke 7:2-10), Peter spoke the word and the lame man was healed "in the name of Jesus Christ of Nazareth" (Acts 3:6). As such, the lame man got up and walked.

If you notice, Peter and John were together. When Jesus sent the apostles (twelve) and the 70 out, they went out in groups of twos (Mark 6:7; Luke 10:1). The Bible says, "Two are better than one; because they have a good reward for their labour" (Ecclesiates 4:9). Torah declares, "At the mouth of two or three witnesses shall he that is worthy of death be put to death" (Deuteronomy 17:6). According to the gospel of Matthew, Jesus said, "For where two or three are gathered together in my name, there am I in the midst of them" (18:20). After Jesus' ascension, the twelve continued to travel in groups of twos (Acts 4:1-13; 8:14; 13:2-5; 15:1-2).

Examination of Acts 3:16

One day as Peter and John were going into the temple to pray, a lame man asked them for "alms." The man looked for one thing but got another. Instead of giving him money, Peter said "look on us" and "in the name [power and authority] of Jesus Christ of Nazareth rise up and walk." The man got up and walked. This is the first recorded healing by an apostle after Jesus' ascension. Later on in his ministry, God used Peter to heal Aeneas (Acts 9:33-34) and raise Tabitha from the dead (Acts 9:36-41).

The crowd marveled and "were filled with wonder and amazement at that which had happened unto him" (Acts 3:10). According to the gospel of Mark, Jesus said, "And these signs shall follow them that believe: In my name, they shall lay hands on the sick, and they shall recover" (16:17-18). Why were the people so amazed when Jesus said, "All things are possible to him that believeth" (Mark 9:23)?

In light of the crowd's reaction, Peter told them that we did not heal him (the lame man) by "our power or holiness" but by faith in Jesus' name. Thus, Peter gave "honour where honour was due" (Romans 13:7). Why were they so surprised?

It was not uncommon for the apostles to go to the temple. For instance, Jesus took them to the temple, where he taught and healed the sick (Mark 11:15-17; 12:35; 14:49; John 8: 2, 20; 10:23-38; 18:20; Matthew 21:14). As an infant, Jesus was dedicated in the temple (Luke 2:1-38). When he was 12 years old, his parents found him in the temple courts (Luke 2:41-47). As an adult, Jesus cleansed the temple (John 2:13-17).

Thought for Acts 3:16

Jesus <u>still</u> heals, and he will heal you (Isaiah 53:5; 1ˢᵗ Peter 2:24). "Heal me O LORD, and I shall be healed; save me, and I shall be saved: for thou art my praise" (Jeremiah 17:14).

Discussion Questions for Acts 3:16

1. What was the lame man's name?

2. How old was he?

3. What was wrong with him?

4. Who were the lame man' parents?

THE EPISTLES OF SHA'UL

("called Paul")

About Paul

What little we do know about the apostle Paul can be found in the Acts of the Apostles and in some of his epistles. We do know that Paul was a Jew (Acts 21:39; 22:3), he was from the tribe of Benjamin (Philippians 3:5), and that Abraham was his father (2nd Corinthians 11:22).

Sha'ul, who is called Paul, was born in Tarsus, and, as he put it, was "a Pharisee, and the son of a Pharisee" (Acts 23:5-6; Philippians 3:5). According to Smith's Bible Dictionary, the Talmud says there were 7 groups of Pharisees. We can only guess which group he belonged to. Paul was one of 6,000 Pharisees during the time of Jesus (Murphy, 1989; p. 582).

As a Pharisee, Paul was well trained (Acts 22:3). No doubt, he was taught Torah and probably read and studied the prophets, psalms, writings, and traditions of the elders. To quote the late Dr. John Arthur Henderson, "Paul spoke 6 languages."

Despite his training, Paul did not receive the gospel of Jesus Christ in the rabbinical school. God gave it to him by revelation so that he would preach it among the Gentiles (Galatians 1:11-12, 15-16). By profession, Paul was a tentmaker (Acts 18:1-3).

Before his conversion, Paul hated and tried to destroy the fledgling (young) Jewish congregation. He consented to the death of Stephen (Acts 8:1, 3; 22:20) and persecuted the church of God (Acts 9:1-6, 21; 22:4, 19; Galatians 1: 13, 23), as he says in 1st Corinthians 15:9, "beyond measure". Paul was extremely violent in his effort to stamp out the church (Acts 26:9-11). How long he persecuted the church is anyone's guess. On reflection, Paul said, "I did it ignorantly in unbelief" (1st Timothy 1:13).

The Lord watched Paul and stopped him in his tracks. One day, the Lord knocked him down (Acts 9:3-4) and said, "Saul, Saul why persecutest thou me" (Acts 9:4; 26:14)? Out of curiosity, Saul said, "Who art thou, Lord" (Acts 9:5; 26:5)? The Lord replied, "I am Jesus whom thou persecutest" (Acts 9:5; 26:15). From this point on, Paul's life changed. God used him to turn the world upside down (Acts 17:6).

It probably never occurred to Paul that he was persecuting Jesus of Nazareth (Matthew 25:41; 2nd Corinthians 8:13). What was on his mind? What was he thinking about? Did he think that he was doing God a service (John 16:2)? Can you imagine how the disciples felt? Can you hear their cries and prayers?

The scripture says, "Touch not my anointed, and do my prophets no harm" (1st Chronicles 16:22; Psalm 105:15). Paul touched God's anointed, and God dealt with him. How, you say? God stopped him in his tracks; Paul was blind for 3-days (Acts 9:8-18) and suffered many things for the kingdom of God (Acts 9:13-15; 2nd Corinthians 11:24-33). When we touch God's anointed, we touch Him.

After his conversion, God made Paul a witness (Acts 26:16-18), put him in the ministry and made him a preacher, an apostle, and a teacher to the Gentiles (Galatians 1:15-16; 1st Timothy 2:7). Paul was anointed: he had all of the counsel of God (Acts 20:29) and a revelation ministry (2nd Corinthians 12:7). Demons knew him (Acts 19:15) and God used him. Paul operated in the gifts of the spirit and spoke in tongues (1st Corinthians 13:1; 14:18). He was a powerful man of God.

God used Paul to heal and perform miracles (Acts 14:8-15; 19:11-12), raise the dead (Acts 20:9-12), baptize (Acts 16:14-

15, 27-33; 19:1-6; 1st Corinthians 1:14-16), and circumcise Timothy (Acts 16:1-3). On one occasion, Paul stopped a man from killing himself (Acts 16:25-28) and a priest from offering a sacrifice to him and Barnabas (Acts 14). To keep him humble, as Paul put it, he "was given…a thorn in the flesh… lest I should be exalted about measure" (2nd Corinthians 12:7). Paul suffered but never complained (2nd Corinthians 11:21-33). A description of Paul can be found in The Acts of Paul and Thecla chapter 1:4-7.

Out of 27 New Testament documents (books and/or epistles), Paul wrote about 50 percent of them. If he is the author of Hebrews, he wrote 14. Out of 13 known Pauline epistles, he is the "sole" author of Romans, Galatians, Ephesians, and the pastoral letters: 1st and 2nd Timothy and Titus. He is, however, the "first" author of 1st and 2nd Corinthians, Philippians, Colossians, 1st and 2nd Thessalonians, and Philemon. Thank God for the wisdom (2nd Peter 3:15) and epistles of Paul of Tarsus (Acts 22:3).

"Destruction and misery are in their ways."

(Romans 3:16)

Introduction to Romans 3:16

This is one of Paul's prison epistles. In the book of Romans, he addressed several issues in regards to Jews and Gentiles. The following question was on the table: Are Jews better than Gentiles? The short of it is "no" because we are all under the power of sin (3:9), and no one is better than the other.

Examination of Romans 3:16

Paul used scriptures to make his case and describe the spiritual condition of Jews and Gentiles. "Destructions and misery" are in the way of the Jew and Gentile because of their lifestyle. Subsequently, Jews are not better than Gentiles because "we are all under sin" (3:9), and "there is no difference between us" (3:22).

Solomon wrote, "For there is not a just man upon earth, that doeth good, and sinneth not" (Ecclesiastes 7:20). Paul punctuated this text when he said, "For all have sinned, and come short of the glory of God" (Romans 3:23). In Messiah, Jews and Gentile are justified by his blood (Romans 5:9) and Christ died for [all of] us (Romans 5:8), as opposed to them (the Jews).

Every time Paul said "they" or "their" in this chapter, he was talking about Jews and Gentiles. No matter who you are "the wages of sin is death; but the gift of God is eternal life through Jesus Christ our Lord" (6:23). We are in this together. Think about it!

Thought for Romans 3:16

Strive to please the Lord. "When a man's ways please the LORD, he maketh even his enemies to be at peace with him" (Proverbs 16:7).

Discussion Questions for Romans 3:16

1. What does the Bible say about corrupt communication?

2. What does the Bible say about swift feet?

3. What does the Bible say about bitterness?

4. What does the Bible say about hell and destruction?

5. Which scriptures did Paul use to make his case?

"Don't you know that you people are God's temple, and that God's Spirit lives in you?"

(1st Corinthians 3:16, Jewish New Testament)

Introduction to 1st Corinthians 3:16

This looks like a simple text, but it is loaded. In 1982, I heard the late Dr. Ern Baxter say that the church at Corinth was in a "moral mess." The congregation was in a moral mess, as she was carnal and full of envy and strife. As such, the church could not fully embrace the things of God and grow (1st Peter 2:3).

Envy and strife probably caused the Corinthians to say, "I am of Paul, I am of Apollos, and I am of Cephas" (1st Corinthians 3:4-5, 22). The Lord's brother said, "For where envying and strife is, there is confusion and every evil work" (James 3:16). To say the least, the Corinthians had a lot of problems and probably did not walk in the Spirit (Galatians 5:16). Paul wrote this epistle in hopes of establishing order in the church.

Examination of 1st Corinthians 3:16

Paul asked a question and made a statement at the same time. In this epistle, Paul told the Corinthians that they were the temple of God. He reiterated this point in 2nd Corinthians 6:16 when he said, "...for ye are the temple of the living God." As human beings, our temple is temporary (2nd Corinthians 4:18; 5:1) and holy.

God dwells in man, as he said, "I will put my spirit within you" (Ezekiel 36:27). The spirit that God puts in us is the Holy Ghost (Luke 24:29; Acts 1:8; 2:4; 6:1-3). When a person receives the gift of the Holy Ghost (Luke 1:15; 4:1; Acts 2:38; 8:16-17; 10:44; 19:1-6), God dwells and walks in him or her (2nd Corinthians 6:16). As the scripture declares, the Most High lives in people, not temples made with human hands (2nd Chronicles 6:18; Acts 7:48; 17:24).

Thought for 1st Corinthians 3:16

Milk is good for you because it helps you to grow. "As new born babes, desire the sincere milk of the word that they may grow thereby" (1st Peter 2:3).

Discussion Questions for 1st Corinthians 3:16

1. Who were the Corinthians?

2. Who was Chloe?

3. What is envy, strife, and division?

4. "Who" is the most high?

"And when one turns to the Master, the veil is taken away."

(2nd Corinthians 3:16, The Scriptures)

Introduction to 2nd Corinthians 3:16

This text will take you back to Exodus 34:20-35. In sum, Exodus 34:20-35 talks about how the Israelites leaders and the children of Israel responded (reacted) to the glow on Moses' face. The "glow" on his face scared them. As such, Moses wore a veil, but when he went before the Lord, he took it [the veil] off.

Moses met with God on Mount Sinai (Exodus 19:20; 24:12-18; 34) by invitation only. At no time did he go up on his own. Moses spent forty days and forty nights in the Lord's presence (Exodus 28:18; 34:28).

When Moses was on the mount, God gave him commandments

(Exodus 19-30; 31:18; 32:14-16), instructions for his people, and spoke to him face-to-face (Exodus 33:11). According to the sacred text, Moses was meek (Numbers 12:1), an intercessor (Numbers 12:3), and faithful in his house (Hebrews 3:1-5). Above all, the Lord was pleased with him (Exodus 33:17).

Examination of 2nd Corinthians 3:16

Because the children of Israel did not accept Y'Shua (Jesus) as Messiah, "when Mosheh [Moses] is being read, a veil lies on their heart" (2nd Corinthians 3:15, The Scriptures). Thus she (Israel) still can see the veil on his face. When she (Israel) repents and "turn to the Lord," the veil will be taken away. Then, God will put his laws in Israel's inward parts, write it in her heart (Jeremiah 31:31-33), and give her a new heart, a new spirit, and fill her with the promise of the Father (Ezekiel 31:26-27; Luke 24:49). Unfortunately, at that time, Israel did not embrace what God had for her.

Thought for 2nd Corinthians 3:16

God is waiting for you. "…repent ye, and believe the gospel."
(Mark 1:15)

Discussion Questions for 2nd Corinthians 3:16

1. What does "turn to the Lord" mean?

2. What is a veil?

3. Who wore a veil?

"Now to Abraham and his seed were the promises made. He saith not, And to seeds, as of many; but as of one, And to they seed, which is Christ."

(Galatians 3:16)

Introduction to Galatians 3:16

Some of the Pharisees that believed (those who accepted Y'Shua as Messiah) taught the brethren (Gentiles), "Except ye be circumcised after the manner of Moses, ye cannot be saved" (Acts 15:1, 5). Their rhetoric (language) caused a flare-up (riff) in the fledging (young) church. Moreover, the Pharisees' teaching disturbed and troubled the minds of the Gentiles (Acts 15:24; Galatians 1:7). Thus, the leaders in the Antioch church (congregation) sent Paul and Barnabas to Jerusalem.

After much discussion and debate, the Holy Ghost moved the apostles and elders to "rule" that Gentiles did not have to get circumcised and keep Torah. Thus, the leadership wrote a letter and sent it by the hands of Paul, Barnabas, Judas, and Silas (Acts 15: 22) to Gentile believers in [the cities] of Antioch, Syria, and Cilicia. Gentiles were "to abstain from meats offered to idols, from blood, from things strangled, and from fornication" (Acts 15:23-29). In Messiah (Christ), our relationship with God is not based on circumcision and Torah per se (Galatians 5:6). Under grace, we are commanded to "love one another" (John 15:12; see Matthew 22:34-40; Romans 13:8-10).

Paul wrote to Gentiles who had converted to "the way" as opposed to converts to Judaism (Acts 19:9, 23; 22:4; 24:14, 22). Based on the tone of this epistle, some Gentiles ignored the Holy Ghost and the directive (letter) from the Jerusalem council: those who did "fell from grace" (Galatians 5:4). As their leader, Paul emphasized that no man was justified by works of Torah (2:16). He rebuked them and challenged their thinking (3:1-5).

Examination of Galatians 3:16

The question is: "Who is Abraham?" Briefly, Abraham was a Hebrew, who obeyed God. He was the first patriarch and Ishmael' (Genesis 16:16) and Isaac' father (Genesis 25:9). Abraham was a man of faith (Genesis 22) and Esau's and Jacob's grandfather. You can read more about his life in Genesis 11:26 through Genesis 25:1-11.

After his father died (Genesis 11), God told Abram to leave his family and kinsfolk (Genesis 12:1). Before he left Haran, God told him, "I will make thee a great nation. I will bless thee, I will make thy name great, and thou shalt be a blessing. I will bless them that bless thee, curse them that curse thee, and in thee shall all the families of the earth be blessed" (Genesis 12:2-3).

When Abram arrived in Canaan, God said, "Unto thy seed will I give this land" (Genesis 12:7). God promised him a "seed" when he was 75 years old and confirmed it when Abraham was 99 (Genesis 17:1-8). The Hebrew writer said, "For when God made promise to Abraham, because he could swear by no greater, he sware by himself" (Hebrew 6:13). God kept his word (promise) and blessed Abraham and Sarah to conceive and have Isaac (Genesis 21:1-8).

When Abram ("exalted father") was 99 years, God changed his name to Abraham ("father of many nations") and gave him the covenant of circumcision (Genesis 17:1-14). Thus Abraham was circumcised when he was 99 years old (Genesis 17:24).

Now, the question is: "Who is the seed of the promise?" Christ is the seed of the promise: he will bruise the serpent's head and destroy the works of the devil (Genesis 3:15; Revelation 12:7-9; 1ˢᵗ John 3:8). Jesus Christ is Abraham's seed (descendant) through Judah. Moreover, anyone, who is in Christ (2ⁿᵈ Corinthians 5:17), is a descendant of Abraham and an heir according to the promise (Genesis 12:1-3; 15:4-6; 17:15-19; Galatians 3:29; 4:28).

Thought for Galatians 3:16

Embrace the seed of the promise. "Therefore if any man be in Christ he is a new creature. Old things are passed away and behold all things become new" (2ⁿᵈ Corinthians 5:17).

Discussion Questions for Galatians 3:16

1. What is a promise?

2. What is faith?

3. Who should we have faith in?

4. How should we live?

5. What is a proselyte to Judaism?

"I pray that from the treasure of his glory he will empower you with inner strength by his Spirit."

(Ephesians 3:16, Jewish New Testament)

Introduction to Ephesians 3:16

This is one of Paul's prison epistles (3:1). Before he was incarcerated (locked-up), Paul spent two years in Ephesus (Acts 19:10). While there, he reasoned with the Jews (Acts 18:19) and preached to everyone in Asia (Acts 19:10). The people in Asia repented, accepted Y'Shua (Jesus) as Messiah, and stopped worshipping idols (Acts 19:23-28). To say the least, the devil was mad! Moreover, God used Paul to baptize (Acts 19:1-6), perform miracles, and heal the sick (Acts 19:11-12). Ephesus was one of the seven churches in Asia (Revelation 2:1-6).

In this epistle, Paul talked about how God revealed the mystery of his will to his holy apostles and prophets by the Spirit (3:5). He asked the Ephesians to pray that God would open his mouth and boldly make known [through him] the mystery of the gospel (6:19).

Paul received the mystery by revelation and had knowledge in the mystery of Messiah. A mystery is a hidden truth that a few people know about. The mystery is that we—Jews and Gentiles—are one in Messiah (Galatians 3:28). As such, the body has many members (nationalities) but is one in Messiah (1st Corinthians 12:12-14). Since "we" are one, there is no wall of partition between us (2:14).

The mystery goes back to a promise that God made with Abraham. "In thee shall all nations be blessed" (Genesis 12:2; 18:18; 22:18). Moreover, God said through the prophet Malachi, "My name shall be great among the gentiles and heathen" (Malachi 1:11)…it is!

Examination of Ephesians 3:16

Paul told the church in Ephesus that he prayed that God would give them strength by his Spirit. "Finally my brethren, be strong in the Lord, and in the power of his might (6:10)." When "we" obey the Lord (Isaiah 1:19) and walk in the Spirit (Galatians 5:16), we will have his strength.

Thought for Ephesians 3:16

The flesh is weak (Matthew 26:41). "Not by might, nor by power, but by my spirit, saith the LORD of host" (Zechariah 4:6).

Discussion Questions for Ephesians 3:16

1. What does Paul mean by "bowing my knees?"

2. What is a saint?

3. Define grace.

4. Which scripture talks about "secret things?"

"Nevertheless, whereto we have already attained, let us walk by the same rule, let us mind the same thing."

(Philippians 3:16)

Introduction to Philippians 3:16

Paul told the church to beware of dogs, evil workers, and the concision (3:2). In his ministry, Y'Shua (Jesus) told people to beware of false prophets (Matthew 7:15), men (Matthew 10:17), the leaven of the Pharisees and Herod (Mark 8:15), covetousness (Luke 12:15), and the scribes (Mark 12:38; Luke 20:46). Embrace what you hear (Hebrews 2:2).

Our apostle (2nd Timothy 1:11) talked briefly about his background, religious zeal, and how he counted "all things dung" for Messiah (3:5-9). Sha'ul (Paul) wanted to know the Lord in the power of his resurrection and in the fellowship of his suffering (3:10).

Examination of Philippians 3:16

Sha'ul (Paul) told the Corinthians to "speak the same thing" in order to avoid division (1ˢᵗ Corinthians 1:10). When Sha'ul (Paul) told the church "to walk by the same rule" and "to mind the same thing," he told them to keep step and to conform to the [same] standard of faith and practice. If we "mind" the same thing, believers will all entertain the things of Messiah. In order to "walk by the same rule" and "to mind the same thing," we must walk in the Spirit (Galatians 5:16) and have the mind of Christ (1ˢᵗ Corinthians 2:16).

Thought for Philippians 3:16

What are you walking in? "…walk in the light, as he is in the light" (1ˢᵗ John 1:7).

Discussion Questions for Philippians 3:16

1. Who is the epistle addressed to?

2. Which king was from the tribe of Benjamin?

3. Who was Benjamin's father?

"Let the message of Christ continue to live in you in all its wealth of wisdom; keep teaching it to one another and training one in it with thankfulness, in your heart singing praise to God with psalms, hymns, and spiritual songs."

(Colossians 3:16, The New Testament in the Language of the People)

Introduction to Colossians 3:16

Sha'ul (Paul) gave the church at Colosse some good advice. For instance, he told them to "seek those things which are above" (3:1), "set your affection on things above" (3:2), not to lie to each other (3:9), and to "forbear and forgive one another" (3:13). Sha'ul wanted the church to put on charity (3:14) and "the bowels of mercies, kindness, humbleness of mind, meekness, and longsuffering" (3:12).

Examination of Colossians 3:16

Allow the word (logos) of God to live in you. This happens when you "receive with meekness the engrafted word of God" (James 1:21). If you are in Messiah (2nd Corinthians 5:17), you have the word living in you (Ezekiel 36:26-27). The scripture declares, "The word of God is quick, and powerful, and sharper than any two-edged sword ... and is a discerner of the thoughts and intents of the heart" (Hebrews 4:12). The word is alive, and like Y'Shua declared, "...the words that I speak unto you, they are spirit, and they are life" (John 6:63). Always let the message of Messiah live in you. Obey the word, as it will do your soul good.

Sha'ul (Paul) wanted the church to willingly teach and share the word with their brothers and sisters in Messiah. As it is written [in Isaiah 54:13], "And they shall be all taught of God" (John 6:45).

The Most High teaches us through his servants (Ephesians 4:11), and He knows how to give us what we need. When we obey the Lord, the word of God, and man of God, as believers, we will come out on top.

In regards to teaching, it is a gift of the Spirit (Romans 12:6-8; 1st Corinthians 12: 27-31; Ephesians 4:11). According to Acts 13:1, there were prophets and teachers in the church in Antioch. Y'Shua (Matthew 5:1), the twelve (Acts 3-5), Paul (2nd Timothy 1:11), Apollos (Acts 18:25), and some of the Pharisees (Acts 15:1, 5) were teachers. To bring the point closer to home, I am a Bible teacher.

Relative to teaching, "nature" is a teacher (1st Corinthians 11:14), bishops should be apt (able) to teach (1st Timothy 3:3), preaching has an element of teaching, and women should not teach without training in scripture (1st Timothy 2:12). The apostle Paul told Timothy that older women should teach younger women [how] to [be] sober, [to] love their husbands and children, [to be] discreet, chaste, keepers at home, good, and obedient to their own husbands (Titus 2:3-5). Above all, the Holy Ghost is a teacher (John 14:26), and those who teach will "receive a greater condemnation" (James 3:1).

Thought for Colossians 3:16

Read the word. "Thy word have I hid in mine heart, that I might not sin against thee" (Psalm 119:11).

Discussion Questions for Colossians 3:16

1. What are the bowels of mercies?

2. What is kindness?

3. What is humbleness of mind?

4. What is meekness?

5. What is longsuffering?

6. Who is longsuffering?

"Now the Lord of peace himself give you peace always by all means. The Lord be with you all."

(2nd Thessalonians 3:16)

Introduction to 2nd Thessalonians 3:16

Paul asked the church to pray for him (3:1). Then, he explained why he wanted and needed their corporate and collective prayers (3:2). As their leader, Paul ordered the church to withdraw from disorderly believers (3:6) and to follow their example (3:7-10). Paul encouraged the Thessalonians to work and to mind their own business. If a brother or sister in Messiah did not work or mind his or her own business (obey Paul's rule), he or she was to be "noted" and left alone (shunned). The crux of Paul's rule was: Do not treat your disobedient brother or sister in Messiah as an enemy but admonish him or her as a brother or sister.

In another epistle, Paul told a congregation (church) not to eat with a brother who was a fornicator, covetous person, idolater, railer, drunkard, or extortioner (1st Corinthians 5:9-11). As believers, we have to be careful as to who we associate with, fellowship with, and hang-out with. Withdrawing from a brother or sister in Messiah may overwhelm and hurt the core of your soul, but it must be done. Only God can give you the strength to do it.

Examination of 2nd Thessalonians 3:16

Paul closed this epistle on a positive note. He wanted the Lord of peace to give the church peace and to be with them.

In regards to peace, Jesus preached peace (Acts 10:36) and people held their peace (Acts 15:13). Peace is a fruit of the spirit (Galatians 5:22), and, before Jesus ascended, he gave the apostles peace (John 14:27). Above all, peace is in the

Holy Ghost (Romans 14:17).

Thought for 2nd Thessalonians 3:16

Do not let the devil fool you. "Be not deceived: evil communications corrupt good manners" (1st Corinthians 15:33).

Discussion Questions for 2nd Thessalonians 3:16

1. What does it mean to "admonish your brother?"

2. What does the Bible say about work?

3. What is a busybody?

4. What is peace?

5. Define lord.

6. Who is the Lord?

THE PASTORAL EPISTLES OF SHA'UL

("called Paul")

"And with controversy great is the mystery of godliness: God was manifest in the flesh, justified in the Spirit, seen of angels, preached unto the Gentiles, believed on in the world, received up into glory."

(1ˢᵗ Timothy 3:16)

Introduction to 1ˢᵗ Timothy 3:16

This chapter opens with a discussion on the office of bishop and the role of a deacon. Brother Paul said, "If a man desires the office of bishop, he desireth a good work" (3:1). Some men desired the office, whereas others could care less. If a man, however, did not meet the qualifications, he could not be a bishop (3:2-7) or deacon (3:8-13). For instance, a bishop or deacon had to be blameless, sober, and, if he were married, able to rule his house and keep his children in line. A bishop had to be vigilant, of good behavior, apt to teach, and patient. In regards to deacons, a deacon must be grave (honest), genuine, able to hold the mystery of the faith, and have a pure conscience. Moreover, a bishop or deacon could not be an alcoholic or in it for the money. The church in Philippi had bishops and deacons (Philippians 1:1).

Examination of 1ˢᵗ Timothy 3:16

Paul shared the mystery of godliness with his son and brother in the faith (1ˢᵗ Timothy 1:2; 2ⁿᵈ Corinthians 1:1). As our apostle declared, "And without controversy great is the mystery of godliness." Thus, there is no need to argue, break-up, form splinter groups (denominations), curse, fight, fuss, hate someone, kill, or scream about it. Truth stands on its own feet!

Thought for 1st Timothy 3:16

What did Jesus say about the Father? He said, "God is a spirit: and they that worship him must worship him in spirit and in truth" (John 4:24).

Discussion Questions for 1st Timothy 3:16

1. When was God manifest[ed] in the flesh?

2. When was God justified in the spirit?

3. When was God seen of angels?

4. When was God preached unto the Gentiles?

5. When was God believed on in the world?

6. When was God received up into glory?

"All scripture is God-breathed and is valuable for teaching the truth, convicting of sin, correcting faults, and training in right living."

(2nd Timothy 3:16, Jewish New Testament)

Introduction to 2nd Timothy 3:16

This is Paul's second letter to Timothy, who was a Jew-tile because he came through a Jewish womb. According to Acts 16:1, his mother was a Jewess and his father was Greek (a gentile). Since Timothy's mother was a Jew, she probably taught him the scriptures when he was a child. If she did not teach him the scriptures, perhaps his Jewish grandfather, uncles, or grandmother did (Deuteronomy 6:4-9)?

Examination of 2ⁿᵈ Timothy 3:16

The Old Testament (OT) and the New Testament (NT) are the scriptures. In comparing the gospels to the Old Testament, the late Dr. James Moffatt (1954) said, "The OT [was] the real bible of the early church." Moreover, whenever you read in the Bible, "For it is written" (Romans 12:19), "as it is written" (Mark 7:6), "as it is written in the prophets" (Mark 1:2), "because it is written" (1ˢᵗ Peter 1:16), and "for thus it is written by the prophet" (Matthew 2:5), the writer is talking about a passage in the OT.

Whenever Jesus and Paul quoted the scriptures, they quoted [from] the Old Testament. For instance, Jesus said, "Search the scriptures" (John 5:39) and "the scripture [see Psalm 82:6] cannot be broken" (John 10:32-35). Jesus quoted (Mark 12:10) and read publicly from the scriptures (Luke 4:16-21). Above all, our faith (belief) in Jesus must be based on scripture. Jesus said, "He that believeth on me, as the scripture [Old Testament] hath said, out of his belly shall flow rivers of living water" (John 7:38).

In regards to Paul, he went in the synagogues and reasoned with the Jews from out of the OT scriptures (Acts 17:1-2). Paul told the church at Corinth, "Christ died for our sins according to the [OT] scriptures; and that he was buried, and that he rose again the third day according to the [OT] scriptures" (1ˢᵗ Corinthians 15:3-4). In a letter to Timothy, Paul said, "Until I come, devote yourself to public reading of Scripture, to preaching, and to teaching" (1ˢᵗ Timothy 4:13, New International Version). The apostle Peter put Paul's epistles on par with the scriptures (2ⁿᵈ Peter 3:16), and [he] declared, "…that no prophecy of scripture is of any private interpretation" (2ⁿᵈ Peter 1:20).

In this passage, Paul said [that] all of the Old Testament (scripture) is God-breathed and inspired by God. Thus, the

OT has God's seal of approval and is profitable (good) for teaching, reproof, correction, and instruction in righteousness, as Paul declared, "That the man of God may be perfect, thoroughly furnished unto all good works" (2nd Timothy 3:17). All scripture point to Y'Shua (Jesus) and are the word of God.

Thought for 2nd Timothy 3:16

Your belief in Jesus must be rooted and grounded in scripture. Jesus declared, "He that believeth on me, as the scripture hath said, out of his belly shall flow rivers of living water" (John 7:38).

Discussion Questions for 2nd Timothy 3:16

1. What did Y'Shua (Jesus) say about the scriptures?

2. Which church (congregation) searched the scriptures daily?

3. Which taught one (disciple) was mighty in the scriptures?

4. Which taught one (disciple) used the scriptures to prove that Y'Shua (Jesus) was Messiah?

THE STAND ALONE
To a Group of Messianic Jews (Hebrews)
Jewish New Testament

"Who were the people, who after they heard, quarreled so bitterly? All those whom Moshe [Moses] brought out of Egypt."

(Hebrews 3:16, Jewish New Testament)

Introduction to Hebrews 3:16

This epistle was written to Jews who had accepted Y'Shua (Jesus) as Messiah. The unnamed Hebrew writer (possibly Apollos) had a good knowledge of and was well acquainted with the scriptures. In this epistle, he (or perhaps she) did a comparison of Moses and Jesus.

In regards to Moses, he was from the tribe of Levi. God used him to deliver Israel from Egypt (Exodus 3:8-22; 20:2) and to give them (Israel) Torah (John 1:17). Moses was meek (Numbers 12:3), "faithful in his house" (Hebrews 3:5), and [he] talked with Jesus on the mount of Transfiguration (Matthew 17:1-9; Mark 9:2-8; Luke 9:28-36)

On the other hand, Jesus was from the tribe of Judah and was the seed of the promise (Galatians 3:16). Concerning Jesus, the prophet Isaiah declared, "…behold, your God will come with vengeance, even God with a recompense; he will come and save you" (Isaiah 35:4). When Jesus was on the earth, he was Emmanuel (Matthew 1:23), the Word made flesh (John 1:1, 14), and the Lamb of God (John 1:29, 36). Jesus was and still is the Savior of the world (Matthew 1:21; Luke 2:8-11; John 4:42; 1st Timothy 4:10; 2nd Timothy 1:10; Titus 3:6; 2nd Peter 3:18; 1st John 4:14). Jesus is an apostle and high priest after the order of Melchizedek, the author of eternal salvation, and the author and finisher of our faith (Hebrews 3:1; 5:6, 10; Psalm 110:4; Hebrews 5:9; 12:2).

Examination of Hebrews 3:16

About 600,000 Israelite men left Egypt on foot, besides women and children according to Exodus 12:37. Dake (1961) estimated that six million people made the exodus from Egypt. Ancient Israel grew from 70 to 75 souls to a mighty nation (Exodus 1:1-5; Acts 7:14).

For ancient Israel, Egypt was not a good place for her because she was a slave (Exodus 3:7-9; Deuteronomy 26:6-7; Acts 7:34). Although the Lord brought her out "with a mighty hand, and with an outstretched arm" (Deuteronomy 26:8; Psalm 136:11-12), after a few months of freedom, she wanted to go back to Egypt (Numbers 14:1-4). Israel went back to Egypt in her heart (Acts 7:39).

No matter what God did for her, she was not satisfied and murmured against Moses, Aaron, and the Lord (Exodus 15:24; 16:2; Numbers 14:2, 22). That generation died in the wilderness (Numbers 14:28-35; 1st Corinthians 10:10).

This passage takes you back to what the late Bishop Dr. Carey Cornish Bowles called the "book-of-the-way-out", which is the book of Exodus. In this particular text, "they" refer to the children of Israel: she heard the voice (sound) of the trumpet and the voice of the Lord (Exodus 19:16, 19). When ancient Israel heard his voice, it frighten (scared) her. In turn, ancient Israel told Moses, "Speak thou with us, and we will hear (obey) but let not God speak to us, lest we die" (Exodus 20:19). She said one thing but did another (Psalm 136).

Thought for Hebrews 3:16

Do not play with or tempt the Lord. The scripture says, "Thy shalt not tempt the Lord thy God" (Deuteronomy 6:16).

Discussion Questions for Hebrews 3:16

1. How did the children of Israel tempt the Lord?

2. How did the children of Israel provoke the Lord?

3. How long did the children of Israel wonder (meander) in the wilderness?

THE EPISTLE OF JAMES

"For where envying and strife is, there is confusion and every evil work."

(James 3:16)

Introduction to James 3:16

It is debatable as to which James wrote this epistle. Did James, the son of Zebedee (Matthew 10:2); James, the son of Alphaeus (Matthew 10:3); or James, the Lord's brother (Matthew 13:56) write it? James, the son of Zebedee, did not write it because he was "killed with the sword" (Acts 12:2). Either James, the son of Alphaeus, or James, the Lord's brother wrote this epistle. No one really knows but church tradition points to the Lord's brother, who is called "James, the Just" (see Boyle, 1990, p75-79; Foxe's Christian Martyrs of the World, 1985, p7; Josephus, Antiquities of the Jews 20.9.1)).

Examination of James 3:16

Brother James told the twelve scattered tribes what envy and strife would lead to. If you are led by and obey the Spirit (Galatians 5:18), you will not allow envy and strife to take control of you. The spirit of envy is a "work of the flesh" (Galatians 5:19-21) and flies in the face of scripture (Hebrews 12:14). Thus, the spirit of envy and strife is intra-psychic as it comes from within (see Matthew 15; Mark 7). James did not want the twelve scattered tribes to become **corinthianized** (carnal, cold hearted, headstrong, selfish, self-centered, or worldly).

Yielding to the spirit of envy and strife is dangerous. For instance, it caused Satan to rebel (Isaiah 14), Cain slew Abel (Genesis 4:8), and Joseph's brothers hated and wanted to kill him (Genesis 37:18-21). The spirit of envy and strife caused Jannes and Jambres to withstand Moses (1st Timothy 3:8), Absalom rose up against his father (1st Samuel 16-18), and Adonijah tried to take the kingdom of Israel by force (1st Kings 1-2).

The spirit of envy moved the king of Egypt to order the Hebrew midwives to kill all Jewish boys at birth (Exodus 1:16-22). Athaliah tried to destroy (kill) all of the royal seed (1st Kings 11:1-3; 2nd Chronicles 22:10) and Saul tried to kill David (1st Samuel 18: 11-12, 17, 21; 19:1-6, 9-10).

The spirit of strife caused Abram and Lot to go their own way (Genesis 13:5-12), Diotrephes rejected the brethren (3rd John 10), and Ammon manipulated and raped his sister (2nd Samuel 13). Strife will cause kingdoms and families to fall (Matthew 12:25; Mark 3:22-26). It caused the apostles to ask, "Who is the greatest" (Matthew 18:1; Luke 22:24)?

If you are in Christ, do not yield to the spirit of envy and strife. If you do, it will hurt you and other people. As the scriptures declare, do not envy the oppressor (Proverbs 3:31), sinners (Proverbs 23:17), evil men (Proverbs 24:17), or your neighbor (Eccles. 4:4). Follow the wisdom and counsel of the apostle Peter and "lay aside all …envies and evil speaking" (1ˢᵗ Peter 2:1).

Thought for James 3:16

Love your brother and thy neighbor (Leviticus 19:18). The scripture declares, "Thou shall not hate thy brother in thine heart" (Leviticus 19:17).

Discussion Questions for James 3:16

1. What is envy and strife?
2. How do you deal with envy and strife?

THE EPISTLES OF PETER

"Having a good conscience; that, whereas they speak evil of you, as of evildoers, they may be ashamed that falsely accuse your good conversation in Christ."

(1ˢᵗ Peter 3:16)

Introduction to 1ˢᵗ Peter 3:16

It is believed that Peter wrote this epistle around A.D. 60. Like Paul, he talked about the husband and wife relationship. What Peter taught was consistent with Paul's teaching (Ephesians 5:22-29; Colossians 3:18-19).

Examination of 1ˢᵗ Peter 3:16

Nero set Rome on fire and accused the church of starting the fire (Halley, 1962). "Nero tortured and burnt Christians charging them with the crime" (Smith's Bible Dictionary, p217). The church suffered persecutions at the hands of civil authorities (Moffatt, 1954). As such, she (the church) was mistreated and talked about for allegedly setting a fire. In light of her plight, Peter tried to encourage her [the church] to be faithful and to "be ready always to give an answer to every man that asketh you a reason of the hope that is in you with meekness and fear" (3:15).

In light of the church's plight, wisdom (1ˢᵗ Corinthians 1:24) cried out: "A soft answer turneth away wrath", "the tongue of the wise useth knowledge aright", and "a wholesome tongue is a tree of life" (Proverbs 15:1-2, 4). No doubt, wisdom's words encouraged her. Peter must have remembered what Y'Shua Messiah told them (the 12), "For by thy words thou shalt be justified, and by your words thou shalt be condemned" (Matthew 12:37).

Thought for 1ˢᵗ Peter 3:16

Suffering is part of the way. "Yea, and all that will live godly in Christ Jesus shall suffer persecution" (2ⁿᵈ Timothy 3:12).

Discussion Questions for 1ˢᵗ Peter 3:16

1. What is hope?

2. What is sanctification?

3. What does Peter mean by "good behavior"?

"As also in all of his epistles, speaking in them of these things; in which are some things hard to be understood, which they that are unlearned and unstable wrest, as they do also the other scriptures, unto their own destruction."

(2nd Peter 3:16)

Introduction to 2nd Peter 3:16

Peter wrote to people of like precious faith in order to "stir up their pure minds." This is his second epistle.

Peter was familiar with Paul's letters, and, no doubt, knew him. For instance, Peter and Paul were at the first church council in Jerusalem (Acts 15), Paul spent 15 days with him (Galatians 1:8), and Peter gave Paul and Barnabas the right hand of fellowship (Galatians 2:9). When Paul saw Peter's hypocrisy, he rebuked him (Galatians 2:10-14; 3:1). Moreover, Peter called Paul our beloved brother and praised God for how he wrote "according to the wisdom given unto him".

Examination of 2nd Peter 3:16

When Paul's letters were read publicly, some people in the local churches (congregations) did not understand his rhetoric (language) and subsequently distorted, misrepresented, and twisted up his words. According to the late A.T. Robertson (2000), "Peter thus puts Paul's epistles on the same plane with the Old Testament." No doubt, Peter believed that Paul wrote as he was moved by the Holy Ghost (2nd Peter 1:21) and [he] counted his [Paul's] epistles as scripture.

Thought for 2nd Peter 3:16

Do not get trapped in your thoughts. "There is a way which seemeth right unto a man, but the end thereof are the ways of death" (Proverbs 14:12).

Discussion Questions for 2nd Peter 3:16

1. Who was the chief apostle?

2. Define unlearned.

3. Define unstable.

THE EPISTLE OF JOHN

"Hereby perceive we the love of God, because he laid down his life for us; and we ought to lay down our lives for the brethren."

(1st John 3:16)

Introduction to 1st John 3:16

Some church historians believe that 1st, 2nd, and 3rd John were written by the apostle John (Mark 3:13-17). We, however, have no biblical-proof for this.

Concerning John, he was one of the twelve and a part of Jesus' inner circle (Luke 9:28-36). John baptized others (John 4:1), received the gift of the Holy Ghost, healed a lame man (Acts 3), and was a traveling evangelist (Acts 4, 5). Our brother was a pillar in the church (Galatians 2:9) and present at the first church council in Jerusalem (Acts 15). The apostle John gave Paul and Barnabas the right hand of fellowship (Galatians 2:9).

The theme of this epistle "is" love. God's love is manifested in what he does (1st John 3:18) and in what he is (1st John 4:18). In light of the theme, "love ye one another" (John 15:12).

Examination of 1ˢᵗ John 3:16

The text says "God laid down his life for us," but it does not say "how" he laid it down. Because God is [a] spirit (John 4:24), he did not have a human body (Numbers 23:19). Once again, the question is: How did God lay down his life for us? God got into a body (Psalm 40:6-8; Hebrews 10:5-9; John 1, 14; 1ˢᵗ John 3:16) and laid down his life for us in Christ (John 1:29; John 10:17-18; 2ⁿᵈ Corinthians 5:18-19).

When God laid down his life for us, he left us an example to follow (John 13:15) and demonstrated the greatest love. As Jesus declared, "Greater love hath no man than this, that a man lay down his life for his friends" (John 15:13). Because God laid down his life for us, we should be willing to "die" for our brother or sister in Messiah. 1ˢᵗ John 3:16 takes us a little deeper into the mystery of godliness (1ˢᵗ Timothy 3:16).

Thought for 1ˢᵗ John 3:16

Love is a powerful gift. "Greater love hath no man than this, that a man lay down his life for his friends" (John 15:13).

Discussion Questions for 1ˢᵗ John 3:16

1. Define perceive.

2. Define brethren.

3. Why did God "lay down" his life for us?

THE REVELATION OF Y'SHUA MESSIAH
(Jesus Christ)

"So then because thou art lukewarm, and neither cold nor hot, I will spue thee out of my mouth."
(Revelation 3:16)

Introduction to Revelation 3:16

Revelation is the last book in our English Bible. Now, the question is: Who wrote the Book of Revelation? Was it John the Baptist (Matthew 3:1), the apostle John (Luke 6:14), a relative of the high priest (Acts 4:6), or a travelling companion of Barnabas (Acts 13:13, 15:37)? John the Baptist did not write it because he died a martyr (Matthew 14:6-11). Tradition points to the apostle John. God told him, "What thou seest, write in a book, and send it unto the 7 churches which are in Asia" (1:11).

Examination of Revelation 3:16

God was not pleased with the Laodiceans because she was lukewarm. A lukewarm person maybe confused (1st Corinthians 14:33), double-minded (James 1:8), and could be trying to serve two masters (Matthew 6:24). He or she may be unpredictable and may have a hard time walking in the spirit (Galatians 5:16). As believers, choose to be either hot or cold (Joshua 24:14-15), as there is no way around it.

Thought for Revelation 3:16

Sin can and will mess you up. "And because iniquity shall abound, the love of many shall wax cold" (Matthew 24:12).

Discussion Questions for Revelation 3:16

1. Who were the Laodiceans?

2. What does it mean to be lukewarm?

3. Define the phrase "I will spue thee out of my mouth."

SOURCES

Birnbaum, D. (1998). Encyclopedia of Jewish concepts. Hebrew Publishing Company: New York.

Book of Judges. In Wikipedia, the free encyclopedia. Retrieved March 27, 2009 from Wikipedia: http://en.wikipedia.org/wiki/Book_of_Judges.

Boyle, I. (1990). The Ecclesiastical History of Eusebius Pamphilus. Baker Book House: Michigan.

Bruce, F.F. (1977). Paul: Apostle of a heart set free. Eerdmans: Michigan.

Cognomen. In Wikipedia, the free encyclopedia. Retrieved March 12, 2009 from en.Wikipedia.org: http://en.wikipedia.org/wiki/Cognomen.

Dake, F.J. (1961). Dake's Annotated Reference Bible. Dake Bible Sales, Incorporated: Georgia.

Exodus Chapter 3. In The New American Bible (2002). Washington, DC: Confraternity of Christian Doctrine, Incorporated. Retrieved June 11, 2009 from USCCB: http://www.usccb.org/nab/bible/exodus/exodus.3htm.

Foxe's Christian Martyrs of the World (1985). Barbour and Company, Incorporated: Ohio.

Halley, H.H. (1962). Halley's Bible Handbook: An

abbreviated Bible Commentary (23rd edition). Zondervan Publishing House: Michigan.

Howard, G. (1995). Hebrew Gospel of Matthew. Mercer University Press: Georgia.

Judges, Book of. In Jewish Encyclopedia (2002). Retrieved March 27, 2009 from Jewish Encyclopedia.com: http://jewishencyclopedia.com/view.jsp?artid=689=J&search=judges.

Matthews, V. (1978). Basic Bible Dictionary. Standard Publishing: Ohio.

Moffatt, J.A.R. (1954). The Bible: A New Translation. Harper Row Publishing, Incorporated: New York.

Murphy, C. (1989). Dictionary of Biblical Literacy. Oliver-Nelson Books: Tennessee.

Phillips, J.B. (1972). The New Testament in Modern English. MacMillan Publishing Company, Incorporated: New York.

Robertson, A.T. (2000). Word pictures in the New Testament Concise Edition (edited by James A. Swanson). Holman Bible Publishing: Tennessee.

Sandel, S. (1978). Judaism and Christian beginnings. Oxford University Press: New York.

Smith, C. (2002). The everyday guide to the bible: A friendly and informative guide to the Old and New Testament. Humble Creek: Ohio.

Genesis Chapter 15. In The New American Bible (2002). Washington, DC: Confraternity of Christian Doctrine, Incorporated. Retrieved June 10, 2009 from USCCB: htpp://www.usccb.org/nab/bible/genesis/genesis 15.htm.

Smith, W. (n.d.). Smith's Bible Dictionary. Holman Bible Publishers: Tennessee.

Stegeman, H. (1998). The library of Qumran: On the Essences, Quran, John the Baptist, and Jesus. William B. Eerdmans Publishing Company: Michigan and Massachusetts.

Stern, D.H. (1989). Jewish New Testament: A translation of the New Testament that expresses its Jewishness (1st edition). Jewish New Testament Publication: Jerusalem.

Strong, J. (n.d.). The Exhaustive Concordance of the Bible. MacDonald Publishing Company: Virginia.

Tanakh: The Holy Scriptures (1985). The Jewish Publication Society: Pennsylvania and Jerusalem.

The Acts of Paul and Thecla. In The Lost Books of The Bible (1979 edition). Bell Publishing Company: New York.

The Amplified New Testament (1958). Zondervan Publishing House: Michigan.

The Nelson Study Bible: New King James Version (1997). Thomas Nelson Publishers: Tennessee.

The New American Bible: The New Testament (1970). P.J. Kennedy and Sons: New York.

The NIV Study Bible: New International Version (1985). Zondervan Publishing House: Michigan.

The Revell Concise Bible Dictionary (1991). Fleming H. Revell Company: New York.

The Revised English Bible (1989). Oxford University Press and Cambridge University Press:Great Britain.

The Scriptures (2000). Institute For Scripture Research: Rhode Island.

The Works of Josephus: New updated edition (1987). Henderickson Publishing, Incorporated: Massachusetts (translated by William Whiston).

Unger, M.F. (1967). Unger's Bible handbook: An essential guide to understanding the Bible. Moody Press: Illinois.

Vines, W.E. (1985). Vine's expository dictionary of biblical words. Thomas Nelson Publishers: Tennessee.

Williams, C. (1966). New Testament in the Language of the people. In The four translations New Testament (parallel edition). Worldwide Publications: Minnesota.

Book II

"For he will finish the work and cut in short in righteousness: because a short work will the Lord make upon the earth."

(Romans 9:28)

In Memory Of
Mother Verlene Gamble Polite

Dedication

To my immediate family and the memory of my precious late father, Charlie Mack Williams; and uncle and former pastor, the late Bishop Dr. Carey Cornish Bowles...if daddy and Uncle Carey only knew!

FORWARD

A few years ago, it looked as if I were on my way out, but the Lord said, "No." Death manifested itself in the form of two heart attacks, but the Lord said, "No." Thanks be to God!

On December 5, 2007, when I was a patient in Halifax Medical Center, a doctor told me, "We were monitoring you on the screen last night: we saw two heart attacks come on you. They left as fast as they came." That doctor and I had a stare-down but when he left the room, I said, "Thank you, Jesus"! All I knew was that I slept well that night.

In this work, I talk about several themes: Who Is The Word, I Can Do, A Brother, Love, Church Folks, The Watchful Eye, Who Fights For Me, Instead, Why, Time, and Try.

I wrote a poem about death because I wanted to put a different face on it and bring a positive light to the subject. As human beings, we know that death is a part of the life cycle (Eccl. 3:1-2; Hebrews 9:25) but have a hard time coming to grips with it. It is hard to come to grips with death because losing a loved is hard, and, if it were not for the grace and mercy of God, the grief would kill us! I thank the Lord that he gives us the strength to move on.

As a general rule, the human family fears death. I am glad that I do not fear death. If I were afraid to die, the devil would take that fear and try to beat and/or scare me to death with it. "God did not give us the spirit of fear" (2nd Tim. 1:11). If you let it, the fear of death will torment you and turn your life upside down (1st Jo. 4:18). Don't fear death. Instead, fear Him who "is able to destroy both soul and body in hell" (Matthew 10:28). Thus, "He that feareth is not perfect in love" (1st John 4:18). Death is (1) the separation of the soul from the body and (2) the separation of men from God (Vine's expository dictionary of biblical words, p 149).

In regard to death, we can find strength in the Old and New Testaments. God does not delight (take pleasure) in the death of the wicked (Ezek. 18:23) as he is longsuffering and does not want anyone to perish (2nd Peter 3:9). In the psalms, it says, "Precious in the sight of the Lord is the death of his saints" (Psalm 116:15). Our death is precious to him!

King Solomon declared, "The righteous hath hope in his death" (Proverbs 14:32). The question is: Why do the righteous (people of God) have hope in his or her death? I believe that we have hope in death because we look for a resurrection (Job 14: 14, 15; Isa. 26:19; Dan.12:2; Hos. 13:14; John 11:24, 25; 1st Co.15:1-58) and to be "caught up to meet the Lord in the air" (1st Thess. 4:17). I believe that we have hope in our death because we look to judge the twelve tribes of Israel (Matt. 19:28), the world and angels (1st Corin. 6:3). The righteous has hope in death because we "look for new heavens and a new earth, wherein dwelleth righteousness (Isa. 65:17; 2nd Peter 3:16), to "inherit the earth" (Psalm 37:11), and to "reign with Messiah for a thousand years" (Rev. 20:4-6). Having hope in death sounds good to me as the day of death is a good thing (Eccl. 7:1).

In the Messianic Scriptures (New Testament), the apostle John said, "We know that we have passed from death unto life because we love the brethren" (1st John 3:14). This is encouraging!

If you die in Christ (2nd Corinthians 5:17), you are blessed. The scripture declares, "...Blessed are the dead which die in the Lord from henceforth: Yea, saith the Spirit, that they may rest from their labours; and their works do follow them" (Revelation 14:13). I believe that that person is blessed because he or she overcame the world (John 16:33; 1st John 4:4; 5: 4, 5) and is resting from his or her labours. A person who dies in Jesus embraces a better hope and was not defeated by the devil. If you die without Christ, you will be lost (John 3:16; 2nd Pet. 3:9). As the psalmist declared, "The wicked shall be turned to hell, and all nations that forget God" (Psa. 9:17).

The apostle Paul said several things about death. For instance,

"...whether we live therefore, or die, we are the Lord's" (Romans 14:7). He told the church at Corinth, "...we shall not all sleep [die]", but we shall all be changed" (1st Corinthians 15:51) and "to be absent from the body, and to be present with the Lord" (2nd Corinthians 5:8). Concerning his own demise, Paul declared, "To me to live is Christ, and to die is gain" (Philippians 1:21).

The Hebrew writer wrote about people who died in the faith (Hebrews 11:1-13). Those people left this physical world and went to a spiritual world (2nd Corinthians 4:18) looking for a better hope. I believe that the better hope that "they" looked for was Jesus.

When John the Baptist saw Jesus, he said, "Behold the Lamb of God, which taketh away the sin of the world" (John 1:29). You must remember that the Lamb had to die, and He did! Jesus did not rejoice per se about dying on the cross but knew that he had to do it (Psalm 40: 6-8; Hebrews 10: 5-10). Jesus declared, "I must work the work of him that sent me, while it is day; the night cometh, when no man can work" (John 9:4). Dying on the cross was a part of his work.

Concerning the death, burial, and resurrection of Messiah, Paul wrote, "…Christ died for our sins, was buried, and rose the third day according to the scriptures (1st Corinthians 15:3-4, paraphrase). Messiah (Jesus) willingly laid down his life because he had the power to lay it down and the power to pick it up again (John 10:18). Why are you so afraid of death when you do not have anything to lose?

If you are in Messiah (2nd Corinthians 5:17), why are you so afraid of death when you should be looking for a better hope? Jesus said, "I am the resurrection and the life: he that believeth in me, though he were dead, yet shall he live" (John 11:25). Death is not the end as it represents a new beginning! If you let the Lord speak to your heart through the word of God, the scriptures will encourage you.

I do not know how long or short my life will be. I just want the Lord to be pleased with me. One day, I look to hear the Lord Jesus say, "Well done thou good and faithful servant" (Matthew 25:21, 23). Above all, I thank God for the precious gift of the Holy Ghost. At least, I will leave the earth with something that I did not come here with. I pray that the "God of the whole earth" (Isaiah 54:5) bless you as you read this book and share what you learn with others.

World without end,

Thomas Williams   March 8, 2010

Daytona Beach, Florida

What am I?

I am a son because I am child of God and a member of the Williams-Brown family.

I am a man [responsible, mature, and of a full age] because I do not act like, talk like, think like, or reason like a child.

I am Christian because I am in Christ and He is in me.

I am a disciple. Why? I am a student-of-scripture, and I allow the Spirit of Truth to lead and guide me into all truth.

I am an apostle and prophet because I was sent out by God. Thus I preach and say what the Lord tells me to say.

I am evangelist and an ambassador for Christ because I take the gospel and represent Christ everywhere I go.

I am a pastor because I look out for and feed the flock of God.

I am a teacher as it is my gift, calling, and profession.

I am an elder in that I am an older man and a leader in the body of Messiah.

I am a minister because I serve others.

What am I? I am a little bit of everything. Above all, I am a servant of God.

To my precious mother

Because the time is so short, I want you to know how I feel about you.

Thank you for bringing a little brother (me) into the world.

Thank you for taking me to Emmanuel Church of Christ, Revival Temple, the Church of the Living God, and to the Evangelistic Glorious Church of God in Christ. I have good memories of those days.

Thank you for praying for me, supporting me in ministry, and for putting up with me.

Thank you for all of the good meals and conversations. Your listening ear then and now still means a lot to me.

Thank you for taking on daddy's religion and for following Uncle Carey into the apostolic churches. I am saved today because of it!

Always know that I love you dearly and wish you long life and good health.

May the grace of our Lord and Savior Jesus Christ be with your spirit.

(This is a modified version of a letter that I sent to my mother in 2008.)

And the Word Is?

The Word is a lamp and a light (Psalm 119:105).

The Word is quick, powerful, and sharper than any two-edged sword and is a discerner of the thoughts and intents of the heart (Hebrews 4:12).

The Word is like a [burning] fire (Jeremiah 20:9) and a hammer (Jeremiah 23:29).

If you are in ministry, you will preach and teach the Word (2nd Timothy 4).

The Word will make you wise unto salvation (2nd Timothy 3:15) and save your soul (James 1:21). Receive and obey the word of God.

The Word is true (John 17:17) and has enduring power (1st Peter 1:23, 25)

Above all, the Word was made flesh (John 1:14) and is one of the 3 that bear record in heaven. (1st John 5:7).

Who is the Word?

"The Word was made flesh and dwelt among us" (John 1:14).

The prophet declared that "he was despised and rejected of men" and was "a man of sorrows" (Isaiah 53:5). He knew and was "acquainted with grief" (Isaiah 53:5).

Because the human family loved darkness rather than light, the Word was lied on, punched, and people spit in his precious face. We called him names, criticized him, and looked for ways to destroy and entrap him.

The Word was beaten beyond recognition (Isa. 50:6; 52:14) but never complained because he wanted to please his Father.

The Word saved us from our sins.

The Word was wounded for our transgressions, bruised for our iniquities, the chastisement of our peace was upon him and with his stripes we are healed (Isa. 53:5).

John the Baptizer called him the Lamb of God (John 1: 29, 36).

The Word is perfect, the author and finisher of our faith, and the author of eternal salvation.

The Word is meek, lowly, humble, and holy.

The Word is our healer, intercessor, guide, leader, and precious teacher.

The Word is high and lifted up, spotless, and is in heavenly places. The Word is in us and with the Father at the same time.

The Word fought the good fight of faith, will come on the clouds, and one day draw the church up to meet him in the air.

Y'shua Messiah, who the world knows as Jesus Christ of Nazareth, is the Word.

We must

There are some things that we must do before we leave the earth. We must seek the Lord while he may be found, praise Him in a dance, and lift up holy hands without wrath and doubt.

We must speak the truth in love, pray without ceasing, and be born again of the water and spirit.

We must walk in the spirit, by faith, and then fight the good fight of faith.

We must trust and obey the Lord, love and pray for others, and work while it is day.

We must preach and teach the truth in love, rightly divide the word of truth, and search the scriptures.

We must try the spirits, put away the filth of the flesh and spirit, and discern between good and evil.

We should willingly give to others and get ready to go back to be with the Lord.

I can do

When I accepted Christ, I repented of my sins, got baptized (in Jesus' name), and received the precious gift of the Holy Ghost.

Thus, in Christ, I can love my wife, my children, and my in-laws.

In Christ, I can raise my children in the fear and admonition of the Lord.

In Christ, I can love my husband and obey and respect him.

In Christ, I can be a person of substance and of faith.

In Christ, I can be faithful until death.

In Christ, I can be faithful in my marriage.

In Christ, I can obey my parents and respect authority.

In Christ, I can forgive others and obey the law of the land.

In Christ, I can operate in the gifts of and walk in the Spirit.

In Christ, I can put on the new man, walk in the newness of life, and put on the whole armor of God.

In Christ, I can live holy, mind my own business, and be at peace with others.

In Christ, I can serve the Lord with gladness and be faithful unto death.

Above all, I can do all things through Christ according to the will and purpose of God.

Simple man

I am a simple man because I want to be.

I am a simple man who loves to preach and teach.

I am a simple who strives to be humble and meek.

I am a simple man who realizes that I am strong but weak.

I am a simple man who tries to be all that he can be.

I am a simple man with a PhD.

I am a simple man who avoids adultery and idolatry.

I am simple man who strives to walk by faith and be what Jesus wants me to be.

I am a simple man who tries not to fuss, let alone cuss!

I am a simple man who honors family and fidelity.

I am simple man with the fruit of the spirit operating in me.

I am a simple man who prays for others and weep.

Above all, I am a simple black man with Jesus in me..

A brother

A brother is a shoulder to cry on and a source to pull from.

A brother is a friend, confidant, and someone that you can have lunch with in a restaurant.

A brother should love you unconditionally and have your best interest in mind.

A brother should be mature enough to forgive and move on.

A brother should be dependable and a man of substance.

A brother will speak the truth in love when he has power from above.

If a brother is a father indeed, he will protect you and his family.

A brother may be strong, but, at the same time, he is weak.

A brother should be someone that you can share good and bad times with.

A brother will laugh and joke with you, but don't assume that he is a joke!

Above all, a brother is a gift from God.

Man

At times, a man will laugh and joke with you, but don't assume he is a joke!

A man may act like a fool, but don't assume that he is a fool.

If you are like John the Baptist, your head might end up on a silver platter.

At times, it seems apparent that some men "act" like they are from another planet.

It is not good for man to be alone. That's why God gave Adam Eve (Genesis 2:18)!

I agree with the apostle Paul in that a man should put away childish things (1st Corinthians 13:11).

Unlike man, God is able and stable.

If a man is in Christ, he is a new creature (2nd Corinthians 5:17).

A man in Christ should not be lazy, and I pray that he is not crazy.

That old church

I remember the sanctuary choir and feeling the Holy Ghost fire.

I remember as a child sitting in the back of the church, clapping, jumping, dancing before the Lord, and crying.

The ministers preached Acts 2:38, prayed for, and loved us.

I remember my mother crying at the altar, but I never knew why she was crying.

I remember crying the night that my mother received the precious gift of the Holy Ghost.

During the winter months, the church was cold but we still felt the power of the Holy Ghost!

The pastor and his wife are gone, but I still remember that old brick building located on 28 Beacon Street in Newark, New Jersey.

Teaching

Teaching is the gift that keeps on giving.

Teaching is a ministry that is not elementary.

Teaching moves the mind and the spirit.

Teaching is a process of self-development and examination.

Teaching is something that unravels as it travels.

Teaching brings might and later on insight.

A mother

A mother will love, protect and feed her children. Like the late C.L. Franklin sang, "A mother loves her children all the time".

A mother will pray for, surprise, and then hug you, but if you get out of line and ignore her correction, she will turn around and whip you!

As long as she has the breath of life in her body, like the weather, your mother will always be there for you.

If you let her be, she will teach and guide you with the help of the Holy Ghost.

A mother who knows Jesus will let him lead her from earth to glory.

All mothers are different but they still love you and me.

(In honor of all mothers in the known world)

I will not sell

I will not sell my soul to the devil for fishes or loaves.

I will not sell my soul to the devil for friends or loved ones.

I will not sell my soul to the devil for fame, fortune, or advantage.

I will not sell my soul to the devil for praise or acceptance by others.

I will not sell my soul to the devil because I am bought with a price (1st Corinthians 6:20).

Thus I will present my body as a living sacrifice, which will be holy and acceptable unto God (Romans 12:1).

Moreover, I will offer up the sacrifice of praise (Hebrew 13:15) and will be led by and walk in the Spirit (Galatians 5:18).

I will be transformed by the renewing of my mind (Romans 12:2).

Above all, I will not sell my soul to the devil because I belong to God and He belongs to me.

I like

I don't like people looking in my glass house.
I just like the house!

Please don't!

A brother is one thing.
A sister is another thing.
But please do not beat up and abuse them!

You have

No matter how gray the sky, no matter how shady the guy,
you still have what it takes to make it!

He doesn't

God chastens those whom he loves, but he does not abuse them.

One of 4 ways

We're going back to be with the Lord one of 4 ways: by translation, death, whirlwind, or by being caught up to meet the Lord in the air. Get ready for the ride up!

We would never

God has to wipe the tears from our eyes. If he didn't, we would never stop crying!

A heart of a son

I cannot pray for my father any more, but I can pray for you. I cannot look at, talk to, or eat with my father any more, but I can look at, talk to, and eat with you.

(In loving memory of Daddy Emerette Luckie Polite)

Are they?

We know that "all scripture is given by inspiration of God", but, what about the various Bible translations. Are they inspired by God?

Words from my precious late father

One day, my father looked at me and said, "Boy, if you ever go somewhere and don't like how the people are treating you, the same door that you walked in is the same door that you can walk out!" This is a rule that I live by.

Would you?

I once worked for approximately nine cents a minute. Now, I work for twelve cents a minute...would you?

Unplanned

I did not plan to substitute teach as long as I did, but I am glad that I had to because I was able to touch students' lives and help shape the face of a nation.

Why?

When Jesus fed the multitudes, he collected the fragments. If we are following his example, "why" do we throw so much food away?

Love

Love is just what it is. Love is patient and it is kind. According to the apostle Paul, love bears all things, believes all things, hopes for all things, and endures all things. Love won't embarrass you or show off. If you look closely, you will see love in a person's eyes and face. If you listen, you can hear love in a person's voice.

Love is reflected in what we do as opposed to what we say. If you embrace and believe the scriptures, you know that God loved the human family because He laid down his life for us through Messiah. Of all of the spiritual gifts, love (unconditional) is the greatest gift. Above all, love is just what it is.

He is not

When a father deliberately tries to sabotage his children's mother, he is not raising his children in the fear and admonition of the Lord.

When a father lies and steals from his children's mother, he is not raising his children in the fear and admonition of the Lord.

When a father tries to turn his children against their mother, he is not raising his children in the fear and admonition of the Lord.

When a father tries to attack the character of his children's relatives, he is not raising his children in the fear and admonition of the Lord.

When a father supports his children when they disrespect and talk back to their mother, he is not raising them in the fear and admonition of the Lord.

When a father uses the police, the courts, and the division of youth and family services to try to bully and control his children's mother, he is not raising them in the fear and admonition of the Lord.

When a father knows that his children are acting out and running away from home and [he] fails to intervene, he is not raising his children in the fear and admonition of the Lord.

When a father is dead-set on trying to hurt and punish his children's mother, he is not raising his children in the fear and admonition of the Lord.

When a father thinks that he is above the law because of his job, he is not raising his children in the fear and admonition of the Lord.

When a father goes forth in a spirit of lies and deceit, he is not raising his children in the fear and admonition of the Lord.

When a father condemns and judges others, he is not raising his children in the fear and admonition of the Lord.

When a father has three separate sets of children, he is not raising his children in the fear and admonition of the Lord.

When a father repeatedly disrespects and tries to terrorize his children's mother, he is not raising his children in the fear and admonition of the Lord.

When a father calls his children names and tries to break their spirits, he is not raising his children in the fear and admonition of the Lord.

When a father tells his daughters that they are going to be whores just like their mother, he is not raising his children in the fear and admonition of the Lord.

(Dedicated to my sister, Alicia Ann Williams, and to all women who have similar stories to tell)

I must

You may not agree with me, but there are a few things that I must do before I go back to be with the Lord. I must:

Fear God and keep his commandments;

Love and forgive others;

Support the weak;

Obey the word of God;

Read, study, and search the scriptures;

Walk in the Spirit, have a pure heart, and clean hands;

Abstain from fleshly lust which war against my soul;

Cry aloud and spare not;

Speak the truth in love, eat healthy, and work out;

Get plenty of rest, sleep, and live holy; and

Fellowship with my brothers and sisters in Messiah, witness to others, and, above all, love the Lord with all my heart, soul, and strength.

Church folks

Some church folks are born again and can live free from sin with the power of the Holy Ghost.

We are in the world but are not of the world.

Unfortunately, some church folks get weak and will lie and spy on you, and, when it's their time to go, they will die on you.

Some of us are great, others are small, and we try not to fall!

Some church folks sing, shout, and try not to doubt.

We fast, pray, and strive to stay in the narrow way.

Some church folks know Jesus, whereas others try to avoid Jesus.

Some church folks go to college in order to gain and pick up knowledge.

Some of us hold degrees in psychology, sociology, and theology.

All of us want to go to heaven but at times hate brother Kevin.

When some church folks give their money, they try not to look funny.

We avoid dope and reach for hope.

As believers, we strive to avoid falling into fornication and adultery.

Above all, all church folks should have a relationship with the "Father of all, who is above all, and through all, and in you all" (Ephesians 4:6).

In loving memory of
Mother Verlene Gamble Polite

I miss seeing you "lifting up holy hands, without wrath and doubting" (1st Timothy 2:8).

I miss your smile and the warmth that comes from you like the sun.

I miss our conversations and your motherly hugs.

I miss seeing and hearing you laugh.

I miss the spirit of motherhood that you walked in.

I miss seeing the love and concern that you had for me.

Boy, do I miss you and Daddy Polite!

Fathers

Fathers change their children's diapers, feed and bathe them.

A father will love and support his children.

Fathers nurture and build their children's character.

Fathers try to be good role models and get along with their children's mother.

Fathers try not to discourage or break their child's spirit.

Fathers teach their sons how to be men, and at times, he will read to them.

Fathers should be emotionally available and a part of their child' life.

If a father is in Christ, he will raise his children in the fear and admonition of the Lord.

Fathers are friendly but they are not their children's friend.

A father must be firm and fair.

A father is a listening ear and a shoulder to cry on.

A father will be all that he can be in Jesus.

Fathers act in the best interest of their children all the time.

Who am I?

Kings and queens ran from me, but they could not hide from me.

You run from me, but I do not run from you.

I take the great, small, and conquer them all.

Enoch bypassed me and Jesus conquered me.

Elijah missed me the first time, but I got him the second time.

The Egyptians and King David can tell you about me.

Depending on what you do, I'll take you at the appointed time or before time.

When it's your time, I'll take you no matter how loud you cry.

I never discriminate as I take men, women, and children.

If you read Paul's letter, you know that "the wages of sin is death."

I'm fearless, tearless, but never careless

One day, I'll be cast into the lake of fire.

Who am I? Guess!

I'm not your friend

I am the father of lies and a murderer. I'll lie to you, but I won't die for you.

I'll get into your dreams and blood stream.

I'll take on the great and small.

I don't care how I deceive or mislead you because all I want to do is destroy you.

I'll act nice then I'll turn around and stab you with a knife.

If you let me, I'll take your mind and make you frown.

I'll come to you in a drug or as a thug.

I'll take your honey and money.

If I can, I'll destroy you and all those around you.

I'll act like I am going your way because all I want to do is throw you away.

I believe in God, but I am still going to hell.

Know that I am not your friend!

A short laundry list of some things that I like to say

1. Humility carries the day.

2. He wrote the ticket.

3. Writing is a process of self-development.

4. Evil has many faces, but yours don't have to be one of them.

5. God is able.

6. You are going to get it one or two ways!

7. Jesus still heals.

8. I need someone to give me a chance, not a handout!

9. You're in my thoughts and prayers.

10. Teaching is a process of self-examination and development.

11. The scriptures cut its' own way.

12. I'd rather suffer for telling the truth than for telling a lie.

13. People make time to do what they want to do.

14. Freedom of speech is a myth.

15. God isn't playing with us.

16. I love you like a son.

17. I can count my friends on one hand.

18. I want my six-pack back.

19. I look to go back to be with the Lord.

20. Teaching is the gift that keeps on giving.

21. I thank God for every breath and every step.

22. I cannot help you if it hurts me.

23. God has veto power over any decision that I make.

24. No matter what you do or say, I still care.

25. Just because you disagree with me does not mean that I am wrong.

26. You reap what you sow.

27. Jesus still hears and answers prayers.

28. How can you stop loving someone?

29. I will not bow down and worship at the altar of mediocrity.

30. There is nothing like being saved on earth.

31. Father, you are too much!

32. People are precious.

33. I am glad that I had a father.

34. I have a good mother.

35. Don't leave earth without the baptism in Jesus' name and the gift of the Holy Ghost!

36. When I look in their faces, I look into the face of the future.

37. Let the Lord lead you like Gideon.

38. Kindness is strength, not a weakness.

39. You are a child once but an adult forever.

40. I may not be the smartest or strongest man, but I'm still a man.

41. We are all that we have.

42. Is it worth your health?

43. There is no expiration date for prayer.

44. Let it go like gas!

45. Silence has its own voice.

46. I thank God for his grace and mercy.

47. Be yourself.

48. I want the Lord to be pleased with me.

49. We are the sum total of our collective experience.

50. My father's death hit me like a virus.

51. The people that we let in are the ones who can do us in.

52. Thank the Lord!

53. This is too much.

54. I am not just a substitute.

55. I get paid the same amount of money no matter what I wear.

56. Come rain or shine, Jesus will take you through this difficult time.

57. The devil is not dead…he just changed clothes!

58. That's too much!

59. Death is where it is.

60. Do what you have to do.

61. Honor your word.

62. Holiness is a way of life, not a denomination.

63. Do your thing.

64. How can you pastor people that you don't know?

65. Trust your instincts.

66. Don't ignore how you feel.

67. They aren't afraid of us, but they are afraid of each other.

68. This is a color purple moment.

69. If we do not speak out, we will suffer the consequences of silence.

That Friend

Some people say in one breath that they love you, but you never hear the first word from them, NOT unless you call, e-mail, visit, or write them. Oh, but, I am so glad that there is a friend that sticks closer than any brother (Proverbs 18:24). Like the weather, he is always there. Know that he loves you and me. He declared, "I will never leave you nor forsake you" (De. 31:6; Hebr. 13:5) and "I am with you unto the end of the age" (Matt. 28: 20). Unlike Judas Iscariot, he will not betray you (Matt. 26:45-50; 27:3; Mark 14:10, 11). Jesus is that friend, who sticks closer than any brother. Thank God for Him!

School

Some of us attend home school, private schools, public schools, and on Sundays, Sunday school.

Depending on your age, you went to elementary, middle, and then high school.

Some of us went to undergraduate, graduate, and professional school.

If you want job training, you can go to a vocational or technical school.

School is a training station and an extension of the family (Proverbs 22:6) and community.

There, children learn how to try words (Job 34:3).

A world without books

I really don't know what the world would be like if we did not have any books. Do you? I think it would be a scary place because some people would sit around and talk all day.

If we didn't have any books in the world, what would blow our minds? Where would we go, and what would we do?

If we didn't have any books in the world, some of us would die inside or may not be alive.

If we didn't have any books in the world, some people would have a hard time relaxing and feeding their minds.

If we didn't have any books in the world, I think that I would be bored with so much free time.

If we didn't have books in the world, some of us would lose our mind.

If we didn't have any books in the world, some of us wouldn't have any place to go and hide.

If we didn't have any books in the world, I wonder what kind of world this would be.

What in the world have we come to?

The rich get richer and the poor get prison. What in the world have we come to?

Some of us live on Wall Street, but most of us live on Main Street. What in the world have we come to?

At night, people walk the streets looking for a place to eat and sleep. What in the world have we come to?

We live in a culture of child abuse, elder abuse, and spousal abuse. What in the world have we come to?

Some people are addicted to drugs, whereas others are trying to be thugs. What in the world have we come to?

Some children disrespect and mistreat their parents. What in the world have we come to?

The United States was founded on religious principles, but we took prayer and discipline out of the public schools. What in the world have we come to?

The Bible says, "For the wages of sin is death" (Romans 6:23) yet we keep on sinning and doing what we want to do. What in the world have we come to?

Jesus said, "I am the way, the truth, and the life: no man

cometh unto the Father, but by me" (John 14:6). Paul preached that "Jesus is the mediator [go between] between God and man" (1st Tim. 2:5). The Hebrew writer declared that Jesus is the mediator of a better covenant (Hebr. 8:6), the new testament (Hebr. 9:15), and the new covenant (Hebr. 12:24). Yet, some of us ignore scripture and teach that "all roads lead to heaven." What in the world have we come to?

Jesus said, "Men love darkness rather than light because their deeds are evil" (John 3:19). What in the world have we come to?

Some of us support what God hates (Proverbs 6:16-19). What in the world have we come to?

Some religious leaders do not practice what they preach (Matthew 23:3). What in the world have we come to?

Some of us disrespect the house of God and have no respect for God. What in the world have we come to?

Some of us do not fear God, let alone the man of God. What in the world have we come to?

Some people enjoy the pleasure of sin (Hebr. 11:24, 25). What in the world have we come to?

Some airline carriers claim that they lost money, but, at the same time, keep charging us more money. What in the world have we come to?

The watchful eye

God is watching you: can't you see, and he knows all about you and me. God sees in the light and in the night. All people are precious in his sight. His eyes are everywhere, beholding the evil and the good (Proverbs 15:3). Rest assured that God is watching you and me (Psalm 8:4)

From me

Jesus said, "Take my yoke upon you, and learn of me; for I am meek and lowly in heart: and ye shall find rest unto your soul" (Matthew 11:29). I don't know how meek, lowly, or humble I am, but you still can learn from me!

Learning

If you keep an open mind, you can learn by observing and being around others. Thus, you can learn from the butcher, the baker, and the candle stick maker. You may not like it, but you can learn from incriminations and recriminations. If you let it, life and nature will teach you some powerful lessons. Above all, you will learn what you want to learn and from what you try to ignore.

As an educator, I believe that all people have the ability to learn and grow. I never worry about what my students cannot do. Instead, I worry about what they won't do! That bothers me, as I see too much talent going down the drain. In our own way, all of us are smart, but, at times, we act like we are in the dark. If you keep an open mind, you will learn and grow.

Who fights for me?

When I am broke, busted, and feel disgusted, who fights for me?

When I am down to my last dime, who fights for me?

When I feel ostracized and criticized, who fights for me?

When someone lies on and cheats me, who fights for me?

When I am treated like a virus, who fights for me?

When my constitutional rights are violated, who fights for me?

When I feel abused by the system, who fights for me?

When I am shut out of the job market, who fights for me?

When my concerns fall on deaf ears and blind eyes, who fights for me?

When I am charged a convenience fee for paying a bill in person, who fights for me?

When I am punished for graduating from college, who fights for me?

War

A war represents a spiritual conflict fought out in the nature. The Civil War is an example of that. A nation will rise against another nation and a kingdom against another kingdom (Matthew 24:7).

Believe it or not, war broke out in heaven (Rev. 12:7). The archangel Michael (Jude 9) and his angels fought against the dragon and his angels. The dragon and his angels were beat down and cast to the ground (Rev. 12:7, 8). Jesus saw Satan fall from heaven as a flash of lightning (Luke 10:18, The Living New Testament).

The devil is on planet earth. He is angry because he knows that he has a short time (Revelation 12:12, 13) and is going to hell (Matthew 25:41). Just in case you did not know, the devil is walking around looking for someone to destroy (1st Peter 5:8). If you're not careful, he'll try to destroy you….the devil is not dead, he just changed clothes!

The human family cannot go to war against the devil with the aid of the air force, army, coast guard, marine corp., National Guard, or navy. The devil is a spiritual being and only God can stop and destroy him. The apostle Paul calls the devil "the prince of the power of the air" (Eph. 2:2) and the "god of this world" (2nd Corinthians 4:4). The devil has power, but he isn't all powerful!

In order to fight the devil and win, you must resist him (James 4:7) and put on and keep on the whole armor of God (Eph. 6:10-18). If you ever take it off, you will quickly learn that you are no match for him.

When the devil attacks you, you are in spiritual warfare: your mind, body, soul and spirit are under attack. If you get weary, wait on the Lord and he will renew your strength (Isaiah 40:31).

The devil is the enemy of our soul and he is at war with you and me. So make sure that you are vigilant of him (1st Peter 5:8). If you let him, the devil will try to destroy and kill you. War is inevitable; so fight the good fight of faith (1st Timothy 6:12).

One

There is only one God, who created all things through Messiah. He alone is the giver and sustainer of life.

Only God can supply all of your needs, save, heal, and deliver you.

God is the only one who can bless and curse you.

There is only one begotten son of the Father.

Jesus died once for our sins.

There is only one Father, Son, and Holy Ghost.

There is only one mediator between God and man.

Jesus is the only author and finisher our faith.

A first

Adam was the first father, humanly speaking.

Eve had one child at a time.

Noah built an ark in obedience to God.

Mary was impregnated by the power of the Holy Ghost.

Judas Iscariot was the only disciple who (betrayed) Jesus for thirty pieces of silver.

There is only one devil but many demons.

As far as I know, Paul was the only apostle who declared all of the counsel of God (Acts 20:27).

Jealous

Cain was jealous because God favored Able' sacrifice over his (Genesis 4: 3-15).

Cain' jealousy got the best of him. Later on, Cain overpowered and killed his brother.

God dealt with Joseph in visions and in dreams (Genesis 37:5-11; 40; 41). Joseph's brothers were jealous and wanted to kill him.

Jacob made Joseph a coat of many colors (Genesis 37:3). Joseph's brothers hated and wanted to kill him.

Absalom felt "entitled" to his father's throne (1st Samuel 13-18). Absalom' rebellion and jealousy got the best of him and later on it destroyed him.

Lucifer wanted to "ascend into heaven, exalt his throne above the stars of God, sit upon the mount of the congregation, ascend above the heights of the clouds, and [to] be like the most High" (Isaiah 14:13, 14). Instead, he was cast down to the ground.

One day, Aaron and Miriam rose up against their younger brother (Numbers 12). God showed up and showed them who was boss.

Korah and his crew rose up against Moses and Aaron. The earth opened up, swallowed them up, and that was the end of them (Numbers 26:9, 10).

Jealousy caused Lot and Abram to go their separate way (Genesis 13:7-12).

Later on, Uncle Abraham pleaded for Lot and God drove the death angel away (Genesis 18:17-33; 19:12-17).

God is what his name is—Jealous (Exodus 20:5; 34:14).

Believe me when I say this because you don't want to experience that part of Him.

When it's all over

When it's all over, Jesus will come on the clouds and draw the church up (Revelation 1:7).

When it's all over, Jesus will come in his glory, sit upon the throne of his glory, and gather all of the nations (Matthew 25:31-46).

When it's all over, there will be a resurrection of the just and unjust (Revelation 20:12-15).

When it's all over, judgment will begin with the house of God (1st Peter 4:17).

When it's all over, the people of God will be changed and caught up to meet the Lord in the air (1st Corinthians 15:51, 52; 1st Thessalonians 4:13-17).

When it's all over, the fullness of the Gentiles will come in (Romans 11: 25-27).

When it's all over, all of Israel will be saved (Romans 11:25, 26)

When it's all over, repentance will be hid from God's eye (Hosea 13:14)

When it's all over, an angel would have preached the everlasting gospel (Revelation 14:6, 7)

When it's all over, the devil will be cast in the bottomless pit, loosed for a season, and cast into the lake of fire (Revelation 20:1, 12, 13).

When it's all over, the human family will be judged (Romans 14:10; 2nd Corinthians 5:10; 1st Peter 4:17, 18).

When it's all over, we will all stand before the judgment seat of Christ (Romans 14:10, 12).

When it's all over, the 12 apostles will judge the 12 tribes of Israel (Matthew 19:28; Revelation 20:4).

When it's all over, the saints will judge the world and angels (1st Corinthians 6:2, 3).

When it's all over, there will be a new heaven and a new earth (Isaiah 65:17; 2nd Peter 3:13; Revelation 21:1).

When it's all over, the meek will inherit the earth (Psalm 37:11).

When it's all over, the goats will be cast into everlasting fire (Matthew 25:41).

(Originally presented on December 31, 2005 at Daytona Deliverance Church of God in Daytona Beach, FL, where Bishop Quinton T. Wallace was pastor and district overseer)

Words

Words come in all shapes and sizes. So, use them wisely.

Words can build you up (Eph. 4:29). Then, turn around and tear you down (Galatians 5:15).

Always use "fitly spoken words" (Proverbs 25:11).

Use words to bless people as opposed to cursing and hurting them (Romans 12:4; James 3:8-10).

The apostle Paul declared, "Don't let any corrupt language come out of your mouth" (Eph. 4:29, paraphrase).

"Death and life are in the power of the tongue" (Proverbs 18:21). Speak life into someone.

Words come in all shapes and sizes. So, use them with the wisdom and humility of Christ.

Children

It is apparent that some children act as if they are from another planet.

Children are tape recorders and will repeat every word that you say.

A child is known for what he or she does (Proverbs 20:11). What is your child known for?

Some children catch the bus, whereas others fuss, and some have the audacity to cuss.

No matter who, what, or where they are, children are truly a blessing from God (Psalm 127:3-5).

Things I like

I like healthy food, a good conversation, and nice clothes.

I like loving and feeling loved by others.

I like seeing love in action.

I appreciate the challenge of turning an enemy into a friend.

I enjoy preaching and teaching and sharing with others.

I like to cook and feed others.

I appreciate the grace and mercy of God.

I like to read and write.

At times, I can appreciate a slice of chocolate cake, with a cold glass of 2 percent milk.

When I can, I like looking at a good movie and program on television.

I like to feel like I am a part of something.

I like feeling good about myself and others.

I like feeling and experiencing the power of the Holy Ghost.

Above all, I like being born again and being able to live free from sin.

Faith

In order to please the Lord, you need faith. It does not take a lot, so use what you got.

Faith starts small and grows.

You can only come to God by faith.

When you have faith, you can speak the truth in love and boldly come before the throne of grace.

You can ask what you will with faith.

You will love and obey the Lord with faith.

When you have faith, you will fear God and keep his commandments.

With faith, you can live holy, seek peace, and offer up the sacrifice of praise.

By faith, you will acknowledge him.

By faith, you will present your body as a living sacrifice.

If you need faith, you can get it by hearing the word of God.

Miracle

To let Pastor Rodney L. Pearson tell it, "A miracle is the supernatural merging on the nature." It was a miracle when Jesus fed the five thousand. It was a miracle when Enoch was translated. It was a miracle when Elijah went to heaven in a whirlwind. It was a miracle when David killed Goliath. It was a miracle when God parted the Red Sea, ended the Civil War, and made the Emancipation Proclamation the law of the land. It was a miracle when God spared the pilot, crew, and passengers on an USAir flight. It was a miracle when then-Senator Barak Hussein Obama was elected president of the United States. It was a miracle when God fed Israel manna from heaven. It was a miracle when God was manifested in the flesh. It was a miracle when Peter walked on water, healed the sick, and raised the dead. It was a miracle when Paul was converted and God used him to turn the then-world upside down. It was a miracle when Jesus healed the sick, raised the dead, and cast out devils. It was a miracle when Jesus turned water into wine. It was a miracle when God spared Moses' and Jesus' life in infancy. It is a miracle when the devil is exposed and defeated. It was a miracle when Samson defeated his enemies. It is a miracle when you can forgive others, pay your bills, and sleep at night. It was a miracle when women got the right to vote and when apartheid ended. It was a miracle when Antwon Q. Fisher shared his story with the known world. It was a miracle when God showed Moses the promise land. It is a miracle when a sinner is called out of darkness into his marvelous light. It is a miracle that we are saved by grace through faith. It is a miracle when good triumphs over evil. It is a miracle that I survived two near heart attacks. It is a miracle when we have people who love and care about us. It is a miracle to grow old. It is a miracle every time God does something for us. It is a miracle when we accept the Lord's will and rely solely on him. I agree with my precious brother "a miracle is the supernatural merging on the nature."

You don't

You don't want to accidentally hurt someone when you can help them.

You don't want to mistreat your brother or sister (Ephesians 4:32), and you certainly don't want to take the mark of the beast (Revelation 13: 11-18).

You don't want to desert your wife or stab someone with a knife.

Above all, you don't want to ignore the voice of the Lord: if you die in your sins, you will be lost.

No matter

No matter how small or tall you are

No matter how weak or strong you are

No matter how slow or quick you are

No matter how intellectual or street-smart you are

No matter how kind or mean you are

No matter how famous and connected you are

You still are no match for God!

Strife

Strife can cause families, friends, nations, and religious organizations to fall.

Strife can cause brothers and sisters to hate and hurt each other.

If you let it, strife will disturb your relationships and could cause you to lose your mind.

Was he?

Jesus healed the sick, raised the dead, and cast out devils. But, was he ever sick?

Be yourself

Instead of trying to be someone else, just be yourself. You'll be healthier for it, and you need to know it.

Instead of trying to be like someone else, just be yourself. God will know it, and your life will show it.

Instead of trying to be like someone else, just be yourself. We all will know it, and your attitude will show it.

Instead of trying to be like someone else, just be yourself. You are one of a kind and no one has your mind.

Instead of trying to be like someone else, just be yourself.

Teaching Tips for Working with African Americans and Other Student Populations: A short laundry list

1. Be ethical and learn and abide by your state's code of ethics.

2. Be flexible in that all students learn differently.

3. Spread yourself around but save something for yourself.

4. Don't destroy their dreams and don't let them destroy yours!

5. Don't be afraid to challenge your students, but don't be surprised when they challenge you! It's going to happen.

6. Lift students up, not put them down. Give them hope because it floats!

7. Get to know your students and let them get to know you. This can be tricky.

8. Always look for ways to help them.

9. When necessary, solicit their advice and feedback.

10. Remember that you are investing in your student's future and yours.

11. Treat students with the same respect that you want from them.

12. Always look for the positive in each situation and/or circumstance.

13. Learn from failure.

(Originally presented on June 5, 2006 during the Advanced Placement Program's Psychology Professional Night in Daytona Beach, FL)

Time

The Bible says that there is "a time to every purpose under the heaven" (Eccl. 3:1). I guess that the text reflects what Solomon saw and experienced in his day. King Solomon didn't say there is a time to steal; a time to return what you stole; a time to work; a time to retire; a time to put people down; a time to build people up; a time to tell a lie; a time to tell the truth; a time to sin; a time to refrain from sinning; a time to get married; a time to get a divorced; a time to look for a job; and a time to stop looking for a job. Yet, we (people in general) do these things all the time. To go back to the text (Eccl. 3:1-8), how will we know when it's a time to be born, to die, to kill, to heal, to love, to lose, to speak, to pluck up, and to refrain from embracing? Time will tell you as it has its own voice and will speak. Think about it.

A few women in scripture

Eve was the first wife and mother.

Sarah and Elizabeth had a child in their old age.

Rebekah was Isaac's wife and the mother of the first set of twins in scripture.

Leah and Rachel were married to Jacob.

Miriam was a leader in the church in the wilderness.

Deborah judged Israel for forty years.

Athaliah took the throne by force and ruled the house of Judah for six years.

Ruth was a faithful daughter-in-law and a wise woman.

God put Esther in place and used her to save his people.

Mary, the mother of Jesus, received the precious gift of the Holy Ghost.

Pontus Pilate's wife was troubled in a dream because of Jesus.

Lydia was a business woman and Christian.

Philip, who was one of the 7, had 4 daughters who did prophesy.

Priscilla taught Apollos the scriptures and was a leader in the church.

Phebe was a servant in the church.

The Ephesians worshipped the great goddess Diana.

Women operate in the gifts of the spirit.

Older women were treated as mothers, whereas the younger women were treated as sisters.

God calls the church his "bride."

Try

You tried and succeeded. Now, thank the Lord.

You tried and failed. Learn from your mistakes and move on.

You tried and grew. Now, just wait and see how the Lord will use you later on.

Your time and season came. Move on and thank the Lord.

You cannot go above try.

(Dedicated to my son in the faith, Gannon Paige Williams, Sr., elder, pastor, and Bible-teacher)

Go Figure

I am certified and highly qualified, but no one wants to hire me...go figure.

I have a bachelor's degree, a master's degree, and a PhD, but no one wants to hire me...go figure.

I have wisdom that comes from experience, but no one wants to hire me...go figure.

When I had a job, I worked hard and tried to do the best job, but no one wants to hire me...go figure.

I believe in and trust God, but no one wants to hire me...go figure.

I am man of God, who strives to please God, but no one wants to hire me...go figure.

I am prepared and ready to work, but no one wants to hire me...go figure.

I love the Lord and people, but no one wants to hire me... go figure.

I love to reach and teach others, but no one wants to hire me...go figure.

I have a relationship with Christ and always try to be nice, but no one wants to hire me...go figure.

Some of us

The Bible says, "Set your affection on things above, not on things on the earth" (Colossians 3:2). At times, however, I think that our affections are misdirected. Some of us are attached to our abilities, cars, children, communities, degrees, denomination, and education. Some of us are attached to our families, friends, gifts, good looks, houses and jobs. Some of us are attached to our life style, money, memories, positions, power, record of good service, reputation, status, and professional titles. As the apostle Paul declared, "...seek those which are above" (Colossians 3:1). We need to direct our affection and everything that we are to Jesus.

Don't do it

Some people want us to beg them for a letter of recommendation in order to get a job.

Some people want us to beg them for a job and later on for a job promotion.

Some people want us to beg them for a place to stay.

Some people want us to beg them for their affection.

Some people want us to beg them for their hand in marriage and for a place in their college.

Some people want us to beg them for their money.

Some people want us to beg them for membership into their thus-and-so.

If you don't ask, you'll never know. All that another person can say is "yes" or "no"!

I know that it is hard, but try not to beg anyone for anything!

ABOUT THE AUTHOR

Elder Thomas Williams received a doctor of divinity in Bible Technicality from the Bowles Bible Institute of Technicality (in 1992) and a PhD in counseling psychology (with a minor in human sexuality) from The University of Iowa in 1998. While in residency at The University of Iowa, Thomas was a graduate instructor of rhetoric (1992-94), a University of Iowa College of Education Fellow (1994-96), a psychology teacher at Saint Ambrose University (1995-96), and an adjunct professor of sociology at Kirkwood Community College (summer 1996). Williams, a native and graduate of the Newark public school system, graduated from Essex County Vocational and Technical High School ("Newark Tech") and the Wilma Boyd Career School in Pittsburgh, PA in 1979 respectively. In 1981, Thomas repented of his sins, accepted Y'Shua (Jesus) as Messiah, and was born again of the water and spirit (John 3:16; Acts 2:38). Thomas Williams was licensed (in 1984) and ordained (in 1988) at Bowles Chapel New Hope Freewill Baptist Church in Roselle, NJ. Thomas is a servant of Messiah and an avid reader, cook, father-figure, public servant, seasoned traveler, student-of-scripture, and a volunteer with College Summit (housed in Washington, DC). Elder Williams lives, works, and attends a church in Daytona Beach, Florida. This is his first publication.